Community-Based Art Education Across the Lifespan

Community-Based Art Education Across the Lifespan

Finding Common Ground

Pamela Harris Lawton

Margaret A. Walker

Melissa Green

Foreword by Olivia Gude

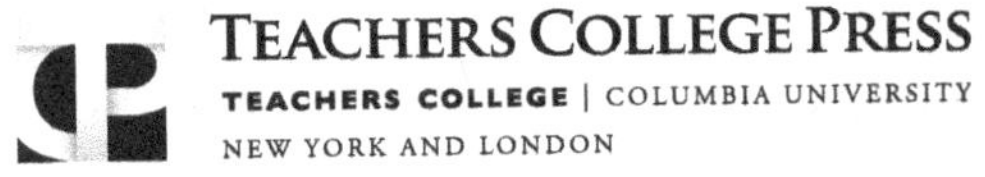

Teachers College Press
TEACHERS COLLEGE | COLUMBIA UNIVERSITY
NEW YORK AND LONDON

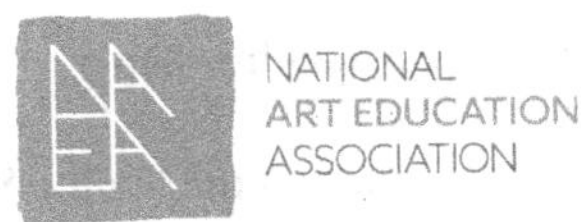

Published simultaneously by Teachers College Press, 1234 Amsterdam Avenue, New York, NY 10027 and National Art Education Association, 901 Prince Street, Alexandria, VA 22314.

Cover photographs taken by Pamela Harris Lawton, Scott P. Mooney, Amelie Haden, and Olivia Davison.

Appendices Curriculum Unit(s) reproduced with permission from Kathryn Rickards, Patrick Carter, Adjoa J. Burrowes, Samantha Strathearn, Buffy Kirby, Erin McArdle.

Library of Congress Cataloging-in-Publication Data

Names: Harris Lawton, Pamela, author. | Walker, Margaret (Margaret Anne), author. | Green, Melissa, 1978- author. | Baca, Judith Francisca, writer of foreword. | Gude, Olivia, writer of afterword.
Title: Community-based art education across the lifespan : finding common ground / Pamela Harris Lawton, Margaret Walker, Melissa Green ; foreword by Judy Baca ; afterword by Olivia Gude.
Identifiers: LCCN 2019011058 | ISBN 9780807761892 (hardcover) | ISBN 9780807761885 (paperback) | ISBN 9780807778005 (ebook)
Subjects: LCSH: Artists and community. | Community arts projects. | Community education. | Art--Study and teaching.
Classification: LCC NX180.A77 H36 2019 | DDC 700.1/03--dc23
LC record available at https://lccn.loc.gov/2019011058

ISBN 978-0-8077-6188-5 (paper)
ISBN 978-0-8077-6189-2 (hardcover)
ISBN 978-0-8077-7800-5 (ebook)

Printed on acid-free paper

Manufactured in the United States of America

To our families, our first teachers; our students, with whom we learn and grow each and every day; and the tireless, unacknowledged, uncelebrated artist-educators who work to ensure that creative expression is attainable, accessible, sustainable, responsive, and inclusive.

Contents

PART II: IMPLEMENTING, CELEBRATING, AND EVALUATING CBAE PROJECTS

Foreword

When I show examples of my collaborative community-based public artworks, I am often asked, "How did you do that? How can I do that type of work myself?" I often find myself at a loss as to how to adequately answer such a complicated question. How can one succinctly explain the many factors that interact when designing, organizing, and collaboratively making a project with many participants? How can one give a sufficiently nuanced account of considerations for the psychological, social, and justice implications of working with diverse communities? How to describe the artist organizer's role in identifying the intertwining of technical and aesthetic means necessary to create a meaningful artmaking process?

Combining their many years of experience as community artists and educators, Pamela Harris Lawton, Margaret Walker, and Melissa Green have provided clear frameworks to address these questions as well as many others in *Community-Based Art Education Across the Lifespan*. Their book offers grounded advice on the process of setting up a community arts project, combining step-by-step practicality with thoughtful observations that identify key ethical and artistic questions associated with each stage of planning and implementation.

Though the focus of the book is community-based art *education*, this book is an important resource for all community arts practitioners because it identifies the responsibility of community artists to teach participants empowering skills (both technical and conceptual) through situated learning experiences. Seeing from the perspective of the artist, the practice and philosophy presented in *Community-Based Art Education Across the Lifespan* encourages educators to be aware that community art projects are not just a matter of transmitting skills and knowledge to participants, but also of understanding participants as co-researchers, engaging in arts-based inquiries that are of significance to themselves and their communities. By linking arts-informed research to methods such as narrative co-inquiry, portraiture as life history, and storytelling, the book expands the conceptual frameworks by which artists and educators can conceive of and shape creative and critical questions, dialogical exchanges, and artmaking activities in their collaborative investigations.

A unique contribution of this book to the literature of community-based art education is its emphasis on multigenerational practice. Making use of psycho-social development theory without being restricted by it, the authors offer fresh insights into how intergenerational communication through art-making can contribute to healing the emotional isolation of our increasingly age-segregated social life.

This book is filled with understated elegant insights that, upon reflection, provide material for years of introspection and elaboration on the nature and possibilities of collaborative arts processes. How might the Freirean notion of generative themes as the identification of limit situations that then call for limit acts, sites of pedagogical inquiry, resistance, and action, also be understood as disorienting dilemmas or as an empowering event, leading to transformational learning? How can such a metaphorical reconceptualization lead to new forms of collaborative artmaking? What might it mean to understand a community arts project as a monumental form of Lev Vygotsky's Zone of Proximal Development in which participants are able to function with a level of sophistication far beyond what each could do alone and then carry these new higher-functioning capacities into future endeavors?

I have been a teacher and community artist for over 40 years and I was fully engaged with this text. I found myself nodding in agreement, frowning in concentration as I considered a fresh perspective, or ironically smiling at pointed advice concerning making plans based on the reality of time constraints. The authors' belief in the significance of community-based artistic practice as an important form of education and of cultural production resonates throughout the text. They speak of community-based art education as *transformative* and as *transgressive*. At first, I was puzzled by their inclusion of transgression in a text focused on fostering empathic understanding and respect for difference. Then it struck me that perhaps the most transgressive act a contemporary artist-educator can make today is to hope and to act, to refuse the master narrative of the inevitability of unbridgeable divides, to continue to collaboratively imagine and make, believing in the transformative value of collective cultural practice.

—Olivia Gude,
Angela Gregory Paterakis Professor and Chair of Art Education,
School of the Art Institute of Chicago (SAIC)

Acknowledgments

We thank Virginia Commonwealth University for the Presidential Research Quest Fund grant and the National Art Education Foundation for the research grant that supported some of the projects discussed in this book.

We are very grateful to our institutions: the Corcoran School of Arts and Design, George Washington University; VCUarts, Virginia Commonwealth University; the Department of Teaching and Learning, Policy and Leadership in the College of Education and the Campus and Community Engagement Office at The Clarice, University of Maryland; and ArtReach at the Town Hall Education Arts Recreation Campus (THEARC) for providing us with time, space, and the opportunity to develop and implement the community-based art education projects referenced here.

We want to express our appreciation to the many communities we have worked with over the years who were willing to share their time, ideas, and space with us to build relationships and learn together through art. In addition, we are deeply grateful to David Walker, who graciously lent us his time and expertise editing our manuscript through various stages; and to our acquisition editors, Noelle de la Paz and Sarah Biondello, at Teachers College Press.

Introduction

The idea for this book surfaced as the three of us were in the midst of teaching our first community-based art education (CBAE) course together. As artist-educators, working collaboratively came naturally and provided opportunities for deeper engagement through art with our students, the local community, and one another around ideas that matter. While each of us had experience with printmaking and with teaching learners from diverse backgrounds, ages, and experiences, none of us had ever created a mammoth woodcut (4 feet by 8 feet) nor used a steamroller as a printing press! The course was complex and involved a variety of experts and specialized materials, but after 8 months of careful planning, it all came together extremely well in the end. Each of us was profoundly transformed by the experience and eager to repeat it in some fashion.

The process itself was empowering and transformed participants' thoughts about their art skills and collaborating with others on complex works of art. Participant feedback reflects this:

> We all worked so very well together! We each took turns carving with the Dremel [rotary] and hand tools. There was not one piece in the whole artwork that we didn't all agree on. It was so symbiotic!

> Collaborating with fellow students, faculty, students from another institution, and members of the community made for a very rich experience, a celebration of diverse perspectives—everyone was made to feel that their contribution was valid.

After our initial collaboration, a whole host of sociopolitical events became front-page news: the Black Lives Matter movement; data breaches at large corporations; state legislation on gay marriage; the Confederate memorials controversy; racial and ethnic hate crimes; disturbing accounts of child abuse and human trafficking; and a plethora of international issues surrounding free speech, diplomatic relations with Cuba, and nuclear weapons agreements with Iran, to name a few. Despite the global connections opened by digital media, contemporary society has become more complex, closed, and divided. Ideologies concerning politics, environmental resources, religion, race, ethnicity, gender, LGBTQ+ identity, age, culture, and education are not only hotly contested issues but also causes that can lead to divisive and often violent actions. These are just a few of the many reasons why CBAE is a critical practice.

WHAT IS CBAE AND WHY SHOULD WE GET INVOLVED?

CBAE provides opportunities for participants from communities of difference and similarity to meet on common ground through art activity and engage in decentered critical discourse through creative collaboration, in their search for creative solutions to difficult community challenges. Through CBAE, participants develop rapport with people and communities they seldom encounter in their daily lives but nevertheless may hold preconceptions about. Establishing rapport is necessary for trust-building; through trust, people are reassured that their voices will be heard and valued and their concerns addressed, making transformation possible. CBAE can foster transformative learning, which "occurs when through critical self-reflection, an individual revises old or develops new assumptions, beliefs, or ways of seeing the world" (Cranton, 1994, p. xii). Learners must be empowered first, before critical self-reflection can take place, and, conversely, empowerment then increases critical self-reflection. CBAE activities allow for an *empowering event*[1] to occur (Lawton, 2004a).

In Freire's (1970) social-emancipatory model of transformative learning, personal and social transformation share a reciprocal relationship, and praxis—the shift between critical self-reflection and action—is pivotal to both equitable personal and societal transformation (Taylor, 1998). Social transformation is a lofty goal, built on hope; without hope, possibilities for transformation are virtually nonexistent. For pre-K–16 educators, CBAE allows learners to make connections between their art education in a classroom setting and its application in the community beyond school, with demonstrable examples of how the arts impact responsible citizenship.

Finally, CBAE fosters a means for intergenerational discourse and learning through ideas that matter. Given that the global population is living longer, the search for new avenues for older adults to exercise *generativity*, the flow of information between generations, and continue to live meaningful lives is crucial to all generations (Andrews, 2000; Erikson, 1959; Erikson, Erikson, & Kivnick, 1986; Wilson, 2016).

Historically in the United States, participation in CBAE has proved to be an especially effective strategy for teaching art/craft skills, connecting diverse groups around common human themes, beautifying spaces, healing unsettled communities, creating opportunities for the silenced to be heard and for the invisible to be seen, and celebrating uniquely traditions and cultural heritage unique to the U.S. Now more than ever, educators need innovative resources to assist them in generating positive classroom/community models. We believe the arts can be a powerful and invaluable tool in narrowing the cultural divide. Using art as a *C.A.L.L.* (see Figure I.1) to action, a language that transcends,

Figure I.1. C.A.L.L: The Goals of CBAE

Connect, collaborate, and create through
Art-based activity that is asset-centered;
Listen to the stories of others to
Learn and build more inclusive and equitable communities and practices.

---

transgresses, and transforms, CBAE stakeholders can express and share their personal voices, lived experiences, and social, moral, cultural, and political concerns for their communities.

The ideas and programs discussed in this book are intended to provide artist-educators with guidance in developing global citizens who will practice empathetic understanding and respect for difference—and for the many ways in which diversity can enrich and transform collective human experience through artistic endeavor. *Community-Based Art Education Across the Lifespan* was written by and for visual art educators, but many of the examples provided integrate the visual arts with the performing arts and other disciplines.

A BRIEF HISTORY OF COMMUNITY-BASED [VISUAL] ART EDUCATION

The term *community* is multifaceted, but most would agree that *community* refers to people or places with at least one common connection, such as language, age, gender, race, ethnicity, religion, ideology, environment, geography, topography, population, location, and so forth. Community also refers to the ways that people with one or more common connections interact with one another. As Lawton (2010, p. 7) notes:

> Definitions of community-based art education include: community art projects that teach art skills, public art that involves interaction among the artist(s) and members of the community, service-learning art projects that unify communities with diverse populations, and outreach programs designed to empower the disenfranchised.

In the United States, CBAE has its roots in social justice and service-learning, beginning with the Settlement House movement at the turn of the 20th century and culminating with the civil rights, peace, and feminist movements of the 1960s and 1970s.

The Settlement House Movement and the Works Progress Administration

The Settlement House movement grew out of the Arts and Crafts Movement in England, which was an arts and social mission to remedy the wrongs of the Industrial Revolution. It was an attempt to improve the quality of life of working men and women, to make culture available to everyone and not just the few, and to reestablish the union of art with craft, lost since the Renaissance. (Efland, 1990, p. 151)

Many proponents of England's Arts and Crafts Movement—spearheaded by William Morris and Walter Crane—visited the United States in the 1890s to garner support for the ideals of the movement, sometimes meeting at Hull House, a settlement house in Chicago founded in 1889 by Jane Addams and Ellen Gates Starr (Efland, 1990). Addams and Starr were influenced by a visit to London's Toynbee Hall, a settlement house for men that provided recreational and social opportunities for upper- and working-class males (Trolander, 1975).

In the United States, most settlement houses were organized in low-income neighborhoods by upper-middle-class women or by religious groups, specifically for the betterment of impoverished immigrant families. These charitable institutions focused on education, cultural activities, and domestic arts and crafts, primarily as a means of developing self-efficacy and social reform. Ellen Gates Starr, an expert at bookbinding, taught her craft at Hull House—probably one of the most celebrated of the U.S. settlement houses, which had the first community school of the arts in the United States and focused specifically on social reform. Privilege and prejudice had no place in Hull House. The doors were open to all, and all were treated with equal respect. The Settlement House movement coincided with the women's suffrage movement, and many of its organizers—indefatigable proponents of legislative change and reform—were leaders in both movements.

By 1920, over 500 settlement houses were in operation across the United States, serving over 12 million European immigrant families. Several of these settlement houses exist to this day, such as Goddard-Riverside in New York City, where Pamela Lawton conducted her Artstories dissertation research. They continue to provide free- or low-cost educational, recreational, and cultural arts opportunities for neighborhood residents.

The stock market crash of 1929 was pivotal in the establishment of the government-run Works Progress/Work Projects Administration (WPA), which provided relief to millions of unemployed workers and thousands of unemployed artists. During the Great Depression of the 1930s and early 1940s, the WPA employed millions of unskilled workers to expand the infrastructure of the United States with bridges, office buildings, highways, dams, and other public works projects (Howard, 1973). In addition, between the years 1935 and 1943, more than 5,000 visual artists and craftsmen were hired as part of Federal Project Number One, which granted them unprecedented freedom to create uncensored public artworks—murals, photography, sculpture, graphic art posters, and so on—many of which continue to grace public buildings today (Adams & Goldbard, 1995). Over 100 community arts centers were established, offering art classes and exhibition spaces to communities across the country (Harris, 1991). The Settlement House movement and the WPA laid the foundation for the broad and varied landscape of community arts organizations that continue to serve neighborhoods throughout the United States today.

The Civil Rights Movement and Beyond

The civil unrest of the 1960s and 1970s created movements that generated the next significant wave of CBAE. The civil rights and Black power movements brought trained artists into urban communities to create street murals and develop exhibitions of paintings and other graphic works in homage to civil rights leaders and ideals. The Coalition of Black Revolutionary Artists (COBRA) formed in Chicago in 1968 after working together on the "Wall of Respect," a mural of historic and contemporary portraits of Black s/heroes representative of the Black power movement. The group's goal was to define a Black visual aesthetic rooted in the positivism of the Black Is Beautiful/Black power movements. It is one of the oldest Black artists' groups in the United States and is active today under the name AfriCOBRA (African Commune of Bad Relevant Artists). Founding member Barbara Jones-Hogu noted:

> We wanted to speak to them and for them, by having our common thoughts, feelings, trials and tribulations express our total existence as a people. We were aware of the negative experiences in our present and past, but we wanted to accentuate the positive mode of thought and action. Therefore, our visual statements were to be Black, positive, and direct with identification, purpose, and direction. (Barbara Jones-Hogu, as cited in WTTW Chicago, PBS, 2016, para. 3)

Many community arts groups arose as a result of the civil rights movement. The San Francisco Neighborhood Arts Program and the Social and Public Art Resource Center (SPARC) in Venice, California, led by Judith Baca, became one of the first citywide community arts projects involving youth from different cultural and economic backgrounds, many from the juvenile justice system, with the goal of fostering cross-cultural dialogue and transforming young lives (Anderson & Milbrandt, 2005; Krensky & Steffen, 2009). These youth art projects became the precursor to similar groups founded during the 1980s and 1990s such as Tim Rollins's Kids of Survival (KOS) group of remedial readers, who used visual art as a means of understanding and connecting to life themes in classic literature, then went on to create community murals of their collaborative conceptions (Paley, 1996).

The Mural Arts Project of Philadelphia, which began as a means of decreasing graffiti, soon grew to include dozens of artists, youths, neighborhood residents, and volunteers, and completed over 2,000 neighborhood murals—all graffiti-free—transforming the Philadelphia landscape and its residents (Golden, Rice, & Kinney, 2003). Also in Philadelphia, the Village of Arts and Humanities, founded by community activist artist Lily Yeh, empowered low-income neighborhoods through the arts and encouraged positive transformation of the physical space.

In the mid-1980s, the Guerrilla Girls, a group of anonymous women artists, took to the streets with posters, books, and performance art to bring awareness to feminist issues in the arts, such as unequal representation in galleries and in the canon of art history. This very brief overview highlights just a few of the players and milestones that contributed to the scope and definition of CBAE.

SUMMING UP, LOOKING AHEAD

As stated earlier, CBAE combines art skill development with social justice, service-learning, and transformative learning practices to empower stakeholders. For the purposes of this book, CBAE focuses on artist-educators working with schools, museums, and arts organizations in multicultural, intergenerational urban and rural communities of learners to foster community and creativity through collaborative artmaking. *Community-Based Art Education Across the Lifespan* will guide artist-educators on how to:

1. Approach a community to work with;
2. Use theoretical frameworks to develop communal understanding, establish rapport, and challenge assumptions;
3. Plan a project in which everyone has a meaningful stake/voice;
4. Dig beneath surface understanding of the creative process and the resulting product to foster a transformative learning experience;
5. Share/publish/exhibit/celebrate the experience within and outside of the community;
6. Establish and evaluate learning outcomes, enduring understandings, and next steps.

NOTE

1. An empowering event becomes possible when stakeholders share stories of experience while collaborating on a creative project, planting the seed of arts-based learning that once nourished can grow and spread to the larger community promoting intergenerational understanding, empathy, and unity.

Part I

PLANNING CBAE PROJECTS

In this part, we develop our definition of community-based art education (CBAE) and those who engage in it through discussion of intersecting practices: socially engaged art, community art, activist art, and art-based service-learning. We then posit conceptual, theoretical, and pedagogical/andragogical frameworks and arts-based research paradigms for the reader to consider in planning and implementing intergenerational CBAE projects. The age-integrated, arts-based curriculum theory Pamela developed through 15 years of CBAE research is presented as a model for designing curriculum (see Appendixes B and C for examples).

This section closes with guidelines for planning and implementing a CBAE project from start to finish: presenting ideas for locating and approaching potential community partners; collaboratively generating themes, issues, or big ideas; and mapping community assets, financial considerations, and the logistics of place, participants, and transportation involved in developing successful projects. Examples connected to the concepts discussed are provided throughout. This section concludes with tenets explaining why CBAE is important, as well as suggestions for navigating privilege and a checklist for what to consider in designing and implementing CBAE projects.

CHAPTER 1

Definitions, Frameworks, and Developmental Theories

This chapter draws on our teaching and research experiences with community-based art education (CBAE) in school, museum, and community settings. It begins with a discussion of terms and definitions related to CBAE; posits a conceptual framework; and discusses relevant psychosocial, cognitive, and artistic development theories. Examples of CBAE programs and research illustrative of the topics discussed are included here and throughout the book to provide context. The following questions guided our thinking:

- What theoretical frameworks should be employed to ensure quality CBAE experiences?
- What sort of learning occurs between educators and stakeholders of all ages engaged in community art practice?
- What educational theories and research methods should be considered in CBAE practice?

TERMS AND DEFINITIONS

Throughout this book we use the term *artist-educator* to refer to art practitioners who facilitate CBAE experiences. We use this term in lieu of "artist," "art teacher," "teaching artist" or "art practitioner" because our focus is on fostering teaching and learning experiences within and across communities and institutions through visual art, and we see this role as best performed by artists who are educators and educators who are artists. Participants in CBAE are referred to here as *stakeholders* instead of "learners" or "participants," because everyone involved in a CBAE project is considered an equal contributor who may impact or be impacted by CBAE practices.

What makes community-based art education (CBAE) different from socially engaged art (SEA) or social practice art, community art, social justice art, and public art is the word *education*. CBAE is primarily about fostering community-based teaching and learning experiences with and through art. The end goal has less to do with protest or sociopolitical change (or adding to an artist's resume or recognition) than with stakeholders learning from one another—about their community as situated in the larger context—while developing art skills, building meaningful connections through artistic collaboration, and inspiring personal and communal transformation in themselves and others. In many instances, this may involve working with underresourced communities and using the arts to bring awareness to inequities experienced by a community, but the work is always asset-centered.

There is certainly much to connect CBAE, SEA, social justice or activist art, and service-learning. CBAE is usually practiced by art educators and teaching artists with formal training in education and/or youth and adult development, thus sharing some common ground with SEA artists, whose interest in "process-based and collaborative conceptual practices" (Helguera, 2011, p. xi) makes them equally at home working with communities and schools as in the studio. Additionally, SEA artists often employ the tools of ethnographers and educators in their work; nevertheless, they consider themselves full-time artists, not educators or social scientists (Helguera, 2011). Social justice or activist art unfolds in the immediacy of public settings and on social media platforms, and typically addresses social inequities; it is practiced by artists, performers, and social activists who use visual art, creative writing, and performance to seek sociopolitical change through public interaction.

Service-learning focuses most directly on the K–16 student and is a means of developing civic responsibility through community engagement. It involves reciprocal, experiential learning through "organized service experiences that meet actual community needs, that [are] integrated into the students' academic curriculum" (Furco, 1996, p.2). Art-based service-learning is closely tied to John Dewey's philosophies regarding "community, democracy, education and art" (Jeffers, 2005, p. 34) and, like CBAE, is reciprocal in nature and built upon a foundation of learning that is transformative. Reflection is an important component of both service-learning and CBAE, as it bolsters understanding, empathy, rapport, and the nurturing of relationships with and among stakeholders. Civic engagement is the end goal of service-learning and is a natural by-product of CBAE, which places special emphasis on relationship-building through story-sharing and artmaking.

"In addition to inspiring aesthetic experiences" (Krensky & Steffen, 2009, p. 8), public art such as commemorative monuments, murals, sculptures, and installations can exist in any medium, and will often honor a historical figure, time, or place; address a social or environmental concern; and be created by commissioned artist(s) for the public domain in areas accessible to all. Community art is closely aligned with public art in that it is publicly accessible; however, community artists design their works for and with a specific community in mind. In most instances, community leaders, businesses, institutions, and grassroots organizations provide input and inspiration for the design of a community-based artwork. CBAE includes aspects of each of the aforementioned art practices, and can encompass public art as well during the exhibition/sharing phase.

According to Krensky and Steffen, "The power of CBAE lies in its ability to be both a context for creating a sense of community and a symbol representing that community's identity and its possible future" (2009, p. 71). Engaging in CBAE allows for stakeholders across the lifespan with a multiplicity of experiences to develop their creative competencies and confidently move toward building more equitable and inclusive communities.

E.R.E.C.T.: CONSTRUCTING A CBAE CONCEPTUAL FRAMEWORK

The five guiding principles below form the basis of our conceptual framework and suggest a best-practices model for organizing, planning, implementing, and assessing CBAE experiences that build upon community assets. These principles are part of any well-considered CBAE project:

1. *Educational.* CBAE provides teaching and learning opportunities for all stakeholders, artist-educators, and the broader community through art experiences, while also promoting narrative co-inquiry, the public exhibition/sharing of understandings and knowledge gained, and art skills, processes, and products.
2. *Reciprocal.* Stakeholders in CBAE establish common ground whereby the contributions and voices of everyone involved are equally heard, appreciated, and considered. Reciprocity is key to developing rapport and trust, valuing diversity and inclusion, and building connections across communities of difference to further understanding and/or meaningful change.
3. *Empowering.* Involvement in CBAE and narrative co-inquiry creates opportunities for self and communal empowerment and efficacy.
4. *Collaborative.* CBAE programs are designed as collaborative creative experiences in which each stakeholder has a meaningful role to play, shares their knowledge, and cooperates in a mutually respectful manner toward the accomplishment of personal and collective goals.
5. *Transformational.* Well-planned CBAE experiences allow for the possibility of an *empowering event* (Lawton, 2004a) to occur that may lead to personal, communal, and societal transformation for the overall benefit of individuals, the community, and the broader society.

CBAE programs should be structured in such a way that stakeholders can engage with each of the principles listed above. CBAE may not always lead to empowerment or transformation, but should always aim toward achieving these ideals.

CBAE AND PSYCHOSOCIAL, COGNITIVE, AND ARTISTIC DEVELOPMENT

Creative, cognitive, and psychosocial development continues throughout our lifetime (Cohen, 2000; Csikszentmihalyi, 1996; Erikson, 1959). Involvement in CBAE is multigenerational and can enrich and enhance our development across the lifespan. Knowledge of the ways in which learners develop cognitively, psychosocially, emotionally, and artistically can aid immeasurably in the design of CBAE curricula by providing a keen understanding of learners' strengths and challenges. Our approach to CBAE takes an eclectic theoretical orientation, as no one theory in its entirety can account for the variety and richness that encompass lifespan learning and development (Santrock, 2010). Given this, our first guiding principle, *education,* utilizes aspects of Erikson's psychosocial development theory to best understand the adult learner; Vygotsky's sociocultural cognitive theory to contemplate how young people construct knowledge; and Bandura's social cognitive theory to consider the connections between cognition, environment, behavior, and the impact of observational learning on CBAE. The artistic development theories of Lowenfeld, Burton, and Kerlavage are examined in designing CBAE curricula for young people, and the theories of creative aging as posited by Csikszentmihalyi and Cohen inform program design for older age and intergenerational CBAE projects. The theories outlined here guide our program planning, interactions, and assessment practices for CBAE. While there are many other developmental theories/theorists, these are the ones we feel are most apt for our definition of and approach to CBAE.

Psychosocial Development Theory

According to Erikson (1902–1994):

> Given a broader, more encompassing view of the life cycle, the arts provide a curriculum that can be enriching throughout every stage of life, offering a broader range of study experience for pupils of varying capacities and potentials. . . . The arts offer a common language and the learning of that language in childhood could contribute to an interconnection among the world's societies. (Erikson, Erikson, & Kivnick,1986, pp. 317–335)

Erikson (1959) postulates an eight-stage psychosocial identity development theory from birth to old age. We include Santrock's (2010) summary of stages 4 through 8:

1. *trust vs. mistrust*—infancy to first year;
2. *autonomy vs. shame/doubt*—infancy (1–3 years);
3. *initiative vs. guilt*—early childhood/pre-school (3–5 years);

4. *industry vs. inferiority*—mid/late childhood (age 6 to puberty). During the elementary school years, children's initiative connects them with a variety of new experiences and ideas. It is a time when the imagination soars. However, for some children, lacking support and encouragement to try new things, confidence and competence lag, and feelings of inferiority can take hold. Educators play a very important role at this stage in building children's enthusiasm for learning and productivity.

5. *identity vs. identity confusion*—adolescence (10–20 years). Individuals are finding out who they are, or want to be, and are grappling with many new and conflicting roles as they transition from childhood to young adulthood. Exploring these roles in a healthy manner with parental support leads to a positive life path. Alternatively, if the identity journey involves unhealthy and delinquent behaviors, identity confusion can result. It is important to note that when Erikson developed his theory, LGBTQ+ and gender-nonconforming individuals were considered "confused." Today, we recognize that gender and identity are fluid constructs, a continuum along which individuals travel, not either/or binary constructs indicating delinquent or unhealthy behavior.

6. *intimacy vs. isolation*—early adulthood (20s, 30s). In this stage, young adults develop intimate relationships with friends and romantic partners. This process is described as finding oneself and giving of oneself to another. If healthy intimate relationships are not formed, isolation may occur.

7. *generativity vs. stagnation*–middle adulthood (40s, 50s). The major concern at this stage is guiding the younger generation (such as one's children) toward a successful path in life, in addition to (or as a part of) developing and living a useful life for oneself. If one experiences feelings of incomplete goals and/or an inability to positively influence the younger generation, stagnation may occur.

8. *integrity vs. despair*—late adulthood (age 60+). In Erikson's final stage one reflects on lived life, and either regards their life as having contributed positively to society or concludes that their life has not been well spent, leading to despair. (p. 44)

Of particular relevance to CBAE and its mission is Erikson's concept of *generativity* in stage 7, middle adulthood: "Generativity is primarily the interest in establishing and guiding the next generation" (Erikson, 1959, p. 103). For continued healthy identity development, adults exercise generativity, that is, contribute to a lasting influence or legacy to help later generations, which can include relationships, creativity, ideas, and products (Wrightsman, 1994). CBAE, with its focus on human experience and life themes that matter to all generations, offers abundant opportunities for adults to engage in generativity, particularly those without ready access to family members of other generations. For our purposes, we will focus on stages 4 through 8 of Erikson's psychosocial development theory as they relate to designing CBAE experiences.

Sociocultural Cognitive Theory

Lev Vygotsky (1896–1934) posited that children construct knowledge (constructivism) based on their social interactions, which lead progressively to the internalization of knowledge. Rather than suggest a stage theory of development, Vygotsky hypothesized that "culture and social interactions guide cognitive development" (Santrock, 2010, p. 47). In Vygotsky's view, knowledge is situated and collaborative, meaning that it "is not generated from within the individual but constructed through interaction with other people and objects in the culture [like art] suggesting that knowledge can best be advanced through interaction with others in cooperative activities" (Santrock, 2010, p. 47), such as intergenerational CBAE programs. Vygotsky believed that children's social interactions through play, and their intergenerational activities with more skilled learners, adults, and peers, were crucial to the advancement of cognitive development because "through this interaction, less-skilled members of the culture learn to use the tools that will help them adapt and be successful in the culture". Additionally, this interaction through social activity, such as artmaking, teaches the developing learner to appreciate knowledge and skills prized within a culture. Vygotsky referred to this phenomenon as the *zone of proximal development* (see Figure 1.1), or "the distance between the actual developmental level as determined by independent problem solving and the level of potential development as determined through problem solving under adult guidance or in collaboration with more capable peers" (Vygotsky, 1978, p. 86).

While the traditional art classroom provides learners with many opportunities to collaborate with more skilled and knowledgeable peers, as well as to learn from their teacher, informal collaborations with multigenerational learners in the school community provide broader and richer possibilities for young learners to construct knowledge and appreciate the role of the arts in society.

Social Cognitive Theory

According to Bandura (2002), social cognitive theory addresses human development, adaptation, and change in a cultural context through three modes of agency: personal, proxy, and collective agency. Agency refers to one's ability to intentionally influence their life circumstances. Successful life functioning requires a blend of all three of these agentic factors. For CBAE purposes we

Figure 1.1. Vygotsky's Zone of Proximal Development

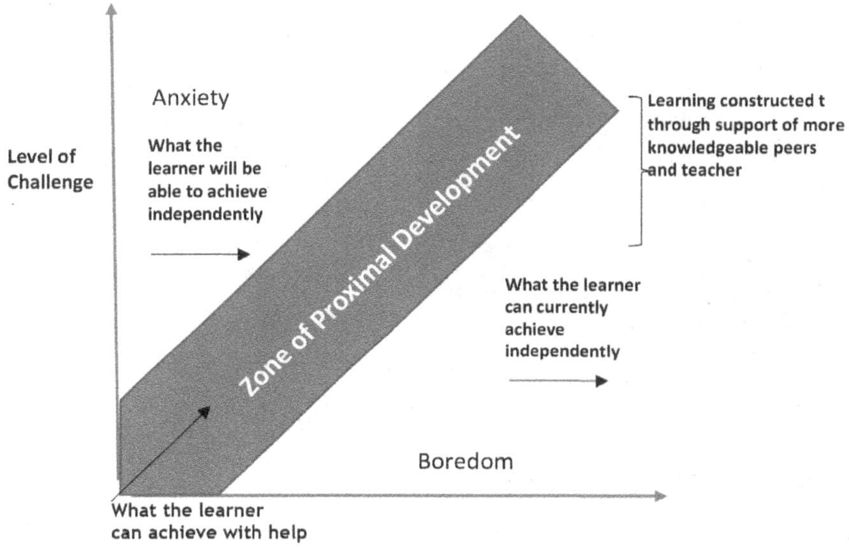

Adapted from edufolios.org/lhswong/2016/09/17/zone-of-proximal-development-vygotsky/

focus on collective agency, whereby "people's shared beliefs in their collective efficacy influence the type of futures they seek to achieve through collective effort; how well they use their resources; [and] how much effort they put into their group endeavors" (Bandura, 2002, p. 271).

Psychologist Albert Bandura believes that behavior, environment, and cognition are the key factors in development (Santrock, 2010). However, Bandura argues that behavior is learned from the environment through the process of observational learning. As Santrock notes, "He proposes that people cognitively represent the behavior of others and then sometimes adopt this behavior themselves" (p. 49). Observational learning occurs frequently within intergenerational activities, and—depending upon where a learner is in their artistic development—the learning may flow in either direction, such as an adult learning an artistic skill mastered by a young person, or vice versa. The collaborative artists' books in Figure 1.2 are a demonstration of the flexibility of teacher–learner roles in CBAE. "Social cognitive theorists stress that people acquire a wide range of behaviors, thoughts, and feelings through observing others' behavior and these observations form an important part of life-span development" (Santrock, 2010, p. 49). Social cognitive theory connects to the reciprocal principle of our E.R.E.C.T framework.

Figure 1.2. Artstories Collaborative Artists' Books

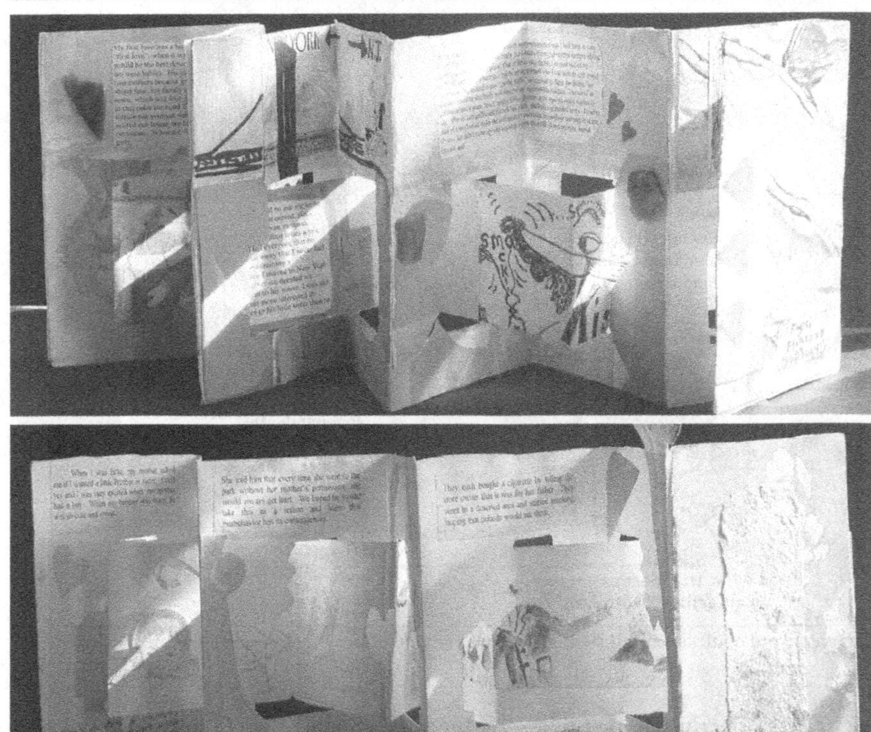

In 2000 Lawton developed and conducted her first CBAE project, Artstories, as part of her dissertation research. The study, an age-integrated, reciprocal arts learning program, involved two mixed groups of older adults and teens. Artstories provided an opportunity for older adults to exercise generativity through story-sharing. The creation of artists' books formed a learning environment in which teaching and learning roles were flexible and reciprocal depending upon the task. For example, the older adults took a leadership role in compiling the stories, whereas the teens took the lead in creating the book forms and compiling the illustrations.

Artistic Development Theories

Viktor Lowenfeld's (1903–1960) seminal text, *Creative and Mental Growth* (1947/1952), which was influenced by the psychoanalytic school of psychology, Piaget's cognitive theory, and German theories on artistic development, theorizes that creativity in children is linked to their cognitive, aesthetic, social, physical, and emotional growth. Lowenfeld proposed a theory of artistic development comprising six progressive stages:

1. Scribble, uncontrolled/controlled naming (ages 2–4)
2. Preschematic (ages 4–6)
3. Schematic (ages 7–9)
4. Dawning realism/gang age (ages 9–11)
5. Pseudorealistic/age of reasoning (ages 11–13)
6. Period of decision/crisis of adolescence (ages 14 and above)

For Lowenfeld the purpose of art education was not the *quality* of the art, aesthetic product, or aesthetic experience, but the *connection* between creative expression and real-world life experiences. Art education should teach children "to grow up more creatively and sensitively and [apply their] experience in the arts to whatever life situations may be applicable" (as cited in Michael, 1982, p. xix). This notion of creative expression as a means of making sense of life and the world is directly linked to the ideological underpinnings of CBAE: "Art connects us to our shared humanity and to our fundamental human need to create" (Krensky & Steffen, 2009, p. 5). Additionally, the aesthetic value of artworks created through CBAE is not as important as the learning and social relationships developed in the process of artmaking.

Lowenfeld's theories are still in wide use today, and exemplify the child-centered approach to art education. More recently, art educators Judith Burton and Marianne Kerlavage have expanded upon Lowenfeld's work. Burton (1980a) speaks of artistic expression as a means of developing the mind; young children experience the world primarily through the senses, and their first forays into artmaking with mark-making tools reflect their kinesthetic development. Artmaking is an activity in which both the mind and the body are actively engaged. This process of developing a visual language to express their relationships with people and objects in their world is a form of *sensory logic*—that is, "the selection and bonding of material and subject matter in early [symbol-making] . . . guided by motor, visual, body and affective responses" (Burton, 1980b, p. 61). Burton (1980a) further elaborates upon the importance of dialogue in artistic development, such as in teacher–student and student–student interactions, which equates with the narrative aspects of CBAE, the sharing of experiences as a form of learning. Marianne Kerlavage's ideas on child development have also been highly influential. We utilize Kerlavage's holistic version of Lowenfeld's stages of artistic development whenever we consider the most appropriate materials, tools, and curricula for youth involved in CBAE projects. Like Lowenfeld (1947/1952) and Burton (1980a, b, c, d), Kerlavage's six stages of artistic development "describe the path that the learner takes in graphic and artistic development and the influences that affect that journey" (Simpson et al., 1998, p. 23). However, Kerlavage's explication of the process of artistic development is more comprehensive, and hinges upon the "interaction of different domains of development, cognitive, social, emotional/moral, physical, language and aesthetic" (Luehrman & Unrath, 2006, p. 7), presenting a more holistic view of the developing learner. Her expanded version of artistic development includes linguistic and aesthetic growth, providing CBAE practitioners interested in transdisciplinary methodologies with highly effective guidelines with which to integrate language-based activities into their curricula.

Kerlavage's stages of artistic development are briefly described in the following sections. The age ranges are not hard-and-fast rules but rather general holistic development guidelines that can vary from learner to learner. An excellent resource for selecting the best materials and experiences based on these ages and stages can be found in Mary Hafeli's (2014) *Exploring Studio Materials: Teaching Creative Art Making to Children,* which specifies teaching and learning experiences that have, through material experimentation and exploration, been shown to engage young minds and to interest and enhance the artistic skill and growth of learners.

Mark-Making Stage. In this stage (ages 2–4), children create accidental, experimental marks, scribbles (Lowenfeld, 1947/1952), or pre-graphic representations (Burton, 1980b), which are characterized by four distinct behaviors: manipulation, uncontrolled marking, controlled marking, and planned or named marking. Rapid growth occurs in each of the developmental domains during this stage. Cognitively, children begin to recognize marks, and make "associations between actions and the creation of the mark" (Kerlavage in Simpson et al., 1998, p. 36). Children also begin to understand the concept of right and wrong, which they draw from their social understanding of how the people who make up their world behave. They start to "experiment with sound and words and discover which ones receive the response they want" (Kerlavage in Simpson et al., 1998, p. 36). Physical growth is quadrupled, in terms of height, from birth to the beginning of this stage, and gross motor skills and coordination increase rapidly. Aesthetically, they show a strong visual attraction to objects, colors, and patterns, based on "their sensory response to the visual world" (Kerlavage in Simpson et al., 1998, p. 37).

Early Symbol-Making Stage. During this stage (ages 4–7), children begin to create representative symbols (schema) for things in the real world, such as tadpole-like forms for humans and animals. By the end of this stage, they will have developed a vocabulary of visual symbols that will later be combined and embellished. In children's art, objects may float in space, unattached to a baseline, and symbols may vary in size, based on importance. Simultaneously, they are learning to create letters and numbers and engage in conversational speech. These diversified communication skills heighten their understanding of the causes and consequences of certain behaviors, and children in this stage learn to self-regulate their behavior. Friendships with other children develop, and they begin to compare themselves with others, noting differences and similarities. These behaviors all contribute to the development of personality traits. Physically, fine motor skills begin to develop, as well as perception of two- and three-dimensional objects. Aesthetically, the art images they produce become less sensory-based and more subject matter-based.

Symbol-Making Stage. This stage (ages 7–9) signals a marked shift in children's development, as they become less egocentric and their sphere of influence broadens to include friendships with peers, the learning of new skills, the rules of game-playing, and how·to share. As a result, their art shifts from depicting "what I do" to "what others do," and complex events involving groups of people begin to appear in their artwork. Sensorimotor control and manual dexterity skills improve, and color choices are noticeably realistic, rather than emotional (Burton, 1980c; Simpson et al., 1998; Lowenfeld, 1947/1952). Human figures and objects are more personalized, and gender is distinct. Multiple baselines appear to give a sense of depth.

As the children's visual vocabulary continues to develop, symbols become more refined, and new symbols are continually added (Kerlavage in Simpson et al., 1998). In their focus to include all pertinent information in their visual narratives, children at this stage devise a system of "rules or graphic principles to solve spatial drawing problems" (Kerlavage in Simpson et al., 1998, p. 44). These rules result in multiple viewpoints, such as x-ray views to see both the outside and inside of structures, bird's-eye views, and so on, all within the same artwork (Burton, 1980c; Kerlavage in Simpson et al., 1998; Wilson & Wilson, 1982).

The thought processes of children in this stage begin to resemble those of adults, but only in terms of concrete information (Kerlavage in Simpson et al., 1998). Spatial understanding increases to include the concepts of time, speed, and distance. They also learn to distinguish between fantasy and reality. Linguistically, their vocabulary has increased to about 14,000 words, making it possible for them to learn art terms and apply them in their speech (Kerlavage in Simpson et al., 1998). Socially and emotionally, children in this stage have a keener understanding of themselves, and are better able to compare themselves with their peers (Kerlavage in Simpson et al., 1998).

Emerging Expertise Stage. Children in this stage (ages 9–11) show an "emerging sense of a need for expertise marked by a move from art as symbolic communication toward art as creative endeavor" (Kerlavage in Simpson et al., 1998, p. 50). Lowenfeld (1947/1952) refers to this as the stage of *dawning realism,* in which children understand how things should look, but have not yet developed the skill to portray people and objects realistically. This can result in frustration and dissatisfaction, as well as (for some) a loss of interest in art altogether. While their drawings may show more detail, the figures will often appear stiff; less attention is given to overall composition, and skill in artmaking appears to regress (Burton, 1980d; Kerlavage in Simpson et al., 1998). Artistic themes focus less on the child's personal world and more on broader "social issues, fantasy, observational drawing and design" (Kerlavage in Simpson et al., 1998, p. 52). Color choices become more subjective and realistic, or may disappear altogether, as children narrow their focus to specific tools that they feel they are more successful with, such as graphite pencils.

Cognitively, this stage exemplifies a move toward abstract thinking based on concrete experiences—an ability to think more logically and to see various solutions to visual problems (Kerlavage in Simpson et al., 1998, p. 53). Socially and emotionally, children in this stage know right from wrong. They also intuit that separate social codes govern the behavior of adults. Acceptance by peers is crucial, and children alter their behavior to fit in. Linguistically, they have an adult capacity for language and an increased understanding of metaphor (Kerlavage in Simpson et al.). There is also a lull in their physical development, which contributes to their frustration in not achieving greater realism in their artworks. Aesthetically, there is still a preference for realistic works, but also an increased appreciation of the expressive and stylistic aspects of some artworks (Kerlavage in Simpson et al., 1998, p. 54).

Artistic Challenges Stage. This stage (ages 11–13) often marks the end of formal art classes for the child, but also a new sophistication in grappling with the challenges involved in making art, together with a shift in focus to the end product, as opposed to the process itself. The child shows a fuller grasp of perspective, including how to create the illusion of three dimensions on a two-dimensional surface. Expression in artwork becomes more important, with a decided preference for drawing from observation (Kerlavage in Simpson et al., 1998). Learners experiment with a wide variety of materials that present artistic challenges.

Cognitively, they are in a shifting space, beginning to move from concrete to abstract thought. This prepubescent stage is also one of cognitive dissonance, as they attempt "to reconcile the differences in their roles as children and their roles as adults . . . causing confusion and a lack of emotional control" (Kerlavage in Simpson et al., 1998, p. 56). Social development is also a source of confusion, as behavioral rules learned in earlier stages are now questioned by the children as part of their transition between childhood and adulthood. Linguistically, children in this stage have a vocabulary of about 30,000 words (Kerlavage in Simpson et al., 1998, p. 57). Physically, their bodies are changing at a rapid rate, which can affect motor skills and artistic ability, resulting in further frustration with artmaking (Burton, 1981; Kerlavage in Simpson et al., 1998). Aesthetically, children at this stage are developing their own artistic style and modes of expression, and show a better understanding of how and why other artists create the works they do (Kerlavage in Simpson et al., 1998).

Artistic Thinking Stage. In the final stage of artistic development (ages 14–17), adolescents have an adult understanding of the world and of the artistic process, and their artwork resembles that of the mature artist (Kerlavage in Simpson et al., 1998, p. 58). Having developed a personal style of artistic expression, they are less susceptible to influence by their peers. They have a broader experience with a variety of art media and methods, and experiment with these tools and knowledge to refine their skills and to explore different ways of expressing their creative message. Cognitively, they are fully capable of abstract and metacognitive thought, enabling them to analyze their artistic ability and "form strategies for moving to a higher level of artistic involvement" (Kerlavage in Simpson et al., 1998, p. 61).

Emotionally, puberty causes stress and anxiety regarding their role as young adults and the need to fit in. A sense of invulnerability can lead to dangerous behavior, with little or no regard for consequences (Kerlavage in Simpson et al., 1998). Socially, there is also much confusion, as adolescents develop both a sense of self and a need to integrate with the larger community; often, "conflict with adult authority arises as adolescents attempt to define their role in an adult world" (Kerlavage in Simpson et al., 1998, p. 61). Language development reaches adult levels. Physically, adolescents reach adult maturity, and the motor skill control lost during puberty returns and is refined; their new manual dexterity shows itself in superior art skills and technique (Kerlavage in Simpson et al., 1998). Aesthetically, adolescents have a better understanding of art from the artist's perspective, and evince a new appreciation of the complexity of both technical and conceptual skills.

Putting It All Together

Developmental stage theories are complex and ever-evolving, but crucial to our understanding of learners' abilities and challenges, and thus to the teaching and assessment strategies of art educators (Luehrman & Unrath, 2006). We recommend that educators familiarize themselves with artistic, cognitive, and psychosocial stage theories as a framework for understanding the general characteristics of learners at various ages and stages, and as a guide to the artistic tools, materials, and experiences that will facilitate the learners' best development.

CBAE AND CREATIVITY

Definitions, categories, and theories of creativity abound (Csikszentmihalyi, 1996; Guilford, 1967; Torrance, 1965; Wallas, 1925). But true understanding of creative genius—and reliable ways of measuring creative thinking— remains elusive. To date, the Torrance Tests of Creative Thinking (TTCT) are still the most effective measure of creative productivity. For our purposes, working mostly with nonprofessional artists, creativity is defined as "a new or unique way of seeing, understanding, or doing something that already exists" (Anderson & Milbrandt, 2005, p. 66). As imagination is a universal human trait, everyone has the capacity to be creative (Anderson & Milbrandt, 2005) with a small *c*. "Creative ability is always there—like a muscle—to be developed and strengthened" (Knight & Schwarzman, 2006, p. xviii); the more you engage with your creative abilities, the more creative you will become. And like Sir Ken Robinson (as cited in Assam, 2009), we believe that "collaboration, diversity, the exchange of ideas, and building on other people's achievements are at the heart of the creative process" (p. 25). In other words, creativity is not a solitary exercise, but occurs within a sociocultural context (Anderson & Milbrandt, 2005; Csikszentmihalyi, 1996). Csikszentmihalyi (1996) describes "big *C*" creativity as "a process by which a symbolic domain [like art] in a culture is changed" (p. 7). Csikszentmihalyi further asserts that "creativity results from the interaction of a system composed of three elements: a culture that contains symbolic rules, a person who brings novelty into the symbolic domain, and a field of experts who recognize and validate the innovation" (1996, p. 6). Each of these elements is "necessary for a creative idea, product or discovery to take place" (Csikszentmihalyi, 1996, p. 6). Participation in CBAE provides stakeholders with collaborative outlets by which to foster and grow creativity, to live more fully, leading to "an outcome that adds to the richness and complexity of the future" (Csikszentmihalyi, 1996, p. 2). This discussion of creativity is important, as it links directly to the fourth principle of our conceptual framework, *collaborative*, and to the fact that our creativity has the potential to grow as we age.

Creative Aging Theories

Now that we have established a conceptual and developmental framework to assist in designing meaningful art experiences for all stakeholders, it is useful to consider the relationship between creativity and aging, particularly the impact of CBAE on stakeholders over age 40. In examining Erikson's psychosocial theory, we recognize that learning and development continue as we age, enhancing the quality of life. Many scholars (Cohen, 2005; Csikszentmihalyi, 1996; Hoffman, 1992) believe that "creative pursuits benefit older adults psychologically, physically, and socially" (Lawton & La Porte, 2013, p. 311). Older adults generally have more time to devote to creative pursuits, as their roles and responsibilities as workers and caregivers diminish (Cohen, 2000). For many, it is during the second half of life that creativity is reawakened, when "age can enhance our intuitive powers for self-expression" (Cohen, 2000, p. 70), unleashing the creative potential that is built on life experience. Cohen (2000) suggests four developmental phases that shape how creativity grows and is expressed in the second half of life:

1. *Midlife reevaluation phase* (age 40–60). At this stage, adults experience a sense of crisis or quest, and seek to make their life work more gratifying through creative endeavor. The capacity for introspection and the desire to create a more meaningful life coalesce powerfully in a renewed capacity for creative self-expression.

2. *Liberation phase* (age 60–70). This phase is marked by a new confidence fueled by psychological and emotional self-understanding, providing the impetus for experimentation. Creativity is driven by the feeling, "If not now, when?" Newfound freedom, due to retirement and the knowledge that what has already been built in life will not suffer from exploring new ventures, drives creativity in this phase.
3. *Summing-up phase* (age 70+). At this phase, we are the "keepers of culture," and creative expression occurs through sharing our story by way of personal storytelling (oral, written, visual, performed), philanthropy, community activism, and volunteerism, as we seek to discover the larger meaning of the story of our lives.
4. *Encore phase* (80s +). At this stage, "creative expression is driven by the desire to make strong, lasting contributions on a personal or community level, to affirm life, take care of unfinished business, and celebrate one's own contribution" (p. 79).

President George W. Bush provides an excellent example of how creativity manifests itself in accordance with Cohen's liberation phase. Having served as president of the United States for 8 years, Bush began painting as a hobby after retirement, stating that he found artmaking "relaxing and he hoped it would inspire others to try new things" (Watkins & Gangel, 2017, para. 3). Over the next few years, his painting skills improved considerably. President Jimmy Carter took up painting and woodworking in the liberation phase and continues to paint and write poetry now that he is in the encore stage (Carter, 2018). Attempting to learn a new discipline late in life—particularly one that others have spent an entire lifetime mastering—may be intimidating for many, but a bedrock of self-confidence drawn from successes in other fields will often spur a restless mind to new and challenging quests. This presents an excellent example of the E.R.E.C.T. principle *empowering*, in which success in a new endeavor promotes self-empowerment and self-efficacy.

Creativity and the Flow State

The concept of *flow* or *being in the zone* is not new. Positive psychologist Mihaly Csikszentmihalyi named and studied the flow state as a result of his fascination with artists and how they work. Csikszentmihalyi's research focuses on the pursuit of happiness and creativity through intrinsic motivation. The flow state is one of intense focus and concentration, and typically occurs when one is engaged in a highly appealing favorite activity (Csikszentmihalyi, 2009). Flow connects with our fifth guiding principle, *transformative*. CBAE experiences can provide time and space for intense creative concentration on both an individual and collective level. When one is in the zone, or flow state, "there is no room in [conscious] awareness for [distractions] conflicts or contradictions" (Csikszentmihalyi, 2009, p. 29).

During this immersive state, the consciousness is full of harmonious experiences; what we feel, wish, and think are all congruously synched (Csikszentmihalyi, 2009). Involvement in creative activities can open a direct path to the flow state and make us feel more fully alive. For flow to occur, one must be engaged in activities that have a clear set of goals that require appropriate responses; these goals must be compatible with one another, produce immediate feedback, and require the use of skills to meet a challenge that is just about manageable. Optimal flow experiences involve a fine balance between one's ability to act and the choices of action open to one (Csikszentmihalyi, 2009). The flow state is most likely to occur in well-designed CBAE experiences, where "goals are clear, feedback relevant, and challenges and skills are in balance, [then] attention becomes ordered and fully invested" (Csikszentmihalyi, 2009, p. 31). Figure 1.3 depicts Csikszentmihalyi's flow concept. Flow directly connects to Vygotsky's concept of the zone of proximal development (Figure 1.1).

To foster the flow state in stakeholders, CBAE experiences need to be well-planned, engaging, and challenging, and require a level of problem-solving slightly above the stakeholder's usual abilities. As part of their assessment process, artist-educators designing CBAE projects need to determine their learners' developmental status as regards artistic skill, level of interest, and motivation, in addition to any personal history with the specific art media and materials to be used. Figure 1.4 illustrates participants in the Carving Out Freedom project engaged in the flow state.

SUMMING UP, LOOKING AHEAD

The theories discussed thus far should be helpful in devising pre/post assessment instruments to ensure that planned activities are appropriate for all

Figure 1.3. Csikszentmihalyi's Flow Model

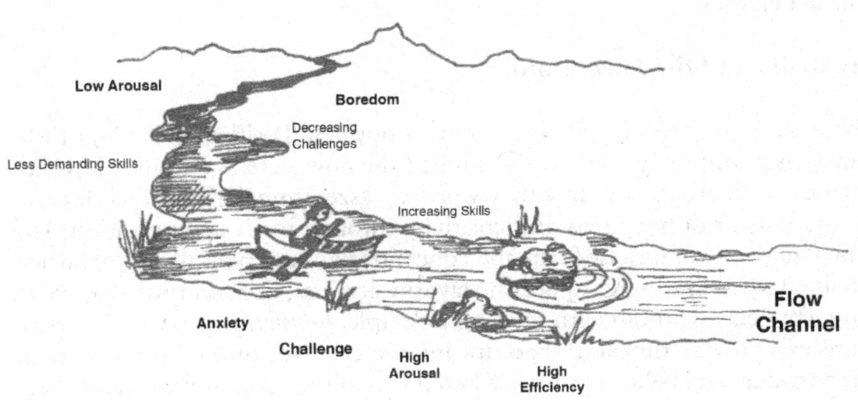

stakeholders involved, and to create an ideal setting for flow moments to occur. A working knowledge of cognitive, psychosocial, and artistic development across the lifespan can be an invaluable tool for devising high-quality CBAE experiences to facilitate learning and enhance creativity. As discussed earlier, learning is the foundation of CBAE. The next chapter examines the educational theories and research paradigms that we believe best demonstrate CBAE teaching and learning strategies at their most effective.

Figure 1.4. Stakeholders in the Carving Out Freedom Project Experience a Flow State of Intense Concentration to Complete Woodblocks Within a Tight Time Frame

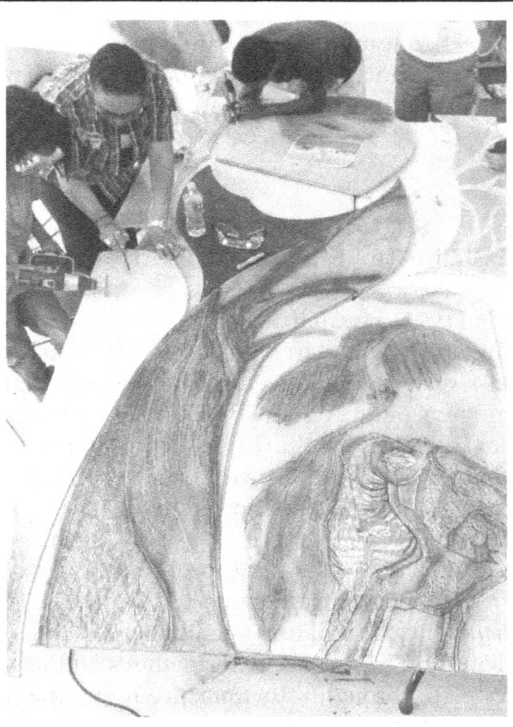

CHAPTER 2

CBAE, Educational Theories, and Research

This chapter examines education theories and research paradigms connected to CBAE and guiding principle one: *educational*. The chapter closes with an age-integrated curriculum theory based on Pamela's research (Lawton, 2004a).

SITUATED LEARNING AND LEGITIMATE PERIPHERAL PARTICIPATION

Lave and Wenger's (1991) research highlights the importance of social situations to learning and to the development of the human mind. Informal learning structures—such as apprenticeships and the sort of observational and experiential learning encounters that CBAE creates—make use of "the tools and representational media that culture provides to support, extend, and reorganize mental functioning" (Pea & Brown, as cited in Lave & Wenger, 1991, p. 11). Lave and Wenger "situate learning in certain forms of social co-participation" (Hanks, as cited in Lave & Wenger, 1991, p. 14), such as the story-sharing that happens in CBAE. Situated learning speaks to the acquisition of knowledge and skill through active engagement in the process. This *legitimate peripheral participation*—such as building one's understanding of the artmaking process through hands-on experience with methods and materials—refers to learning that takes place through actual practice under the limited guidance of an expert (Lave & Wenger, 1991; Vygotsky, 1978). Legitimate peripheral participation opens avenues to understanding through growing involvement, leading to the potential for full participation. Learning is not a solitary endeavor but a collaborative one, a form of social practice "taking place in a participation framework that includes the perspectives of other co-participants" and the teacher (Hanks, as cited in Lave & Wenger, 1991, p. 15). This concept of "learning as increasing participation in communities of practice" suggests "a very explicit focus on the person, but as person-in-the-world, as a member of a sociocultural community" (Lave & Wenger, 1991, pp. 49–52). Legitimate peripheral participation is an analytical viewpoint—not a teaching strategy or technique, but a way of understanding learning (Lave & Wenger, 1991, p. 40). The concept of situated learning has direct connections to Vygotsky's sociocultural learning, Dewey's experiential learning, and Bandura's social cognitive theory of learning through observation.

EXPERIENTIAL LEARNING

Dewey's (1938) progressive education theories are rooted in the concept of learning through hands-on, lived experience of personal and social relevance. In art education, experiential learning connects to child-centered (Lowenfeld, 1947/1952), constructivist (Vygotsky, 1978) pedagogies, whereby the learner makes meaning and develops art skills through exploration and experimentation with art materials. Theories of adult learning, or andragogy, are based on critical reflection of life experience, resulting in a form of self-directed learning (Knowles, 1975; Kolb, 1984). Because CBAE is an informal approach to teaching and learning, it provides opportunities for experiential learning across the lifespan. Experiential learning supports metacognitive reflection, allowing the learner to "analyze their own experience, identify their characteristic assumptions and belief systems, and scrutinize the origins, validity, and consequences of their ideas" (Michelson, 2015, p. 29). Figure 2.1 depicts stakeholders engaged in critical reflection through collaborative artmaking. This critical, metacognitive reflection within a collaborative, creative, and social context makes *empowerment* and *transformation*—two guiding principles of our CBAE conceptual framework—possible.

TRANSFORMATIVE LEARNING

Meaning Perspectives

Jack Mezirow (1923–2014) conceived of the transformative learning theory of adult education in 1978, based on a U.S. study of women returning to college after a long hiatus from school. Transformative learning "involves reflectively transforming the beliefs, attitudes, opinions, and emotional reactions that constitute our meaning schemes, or transforming our meaning perspectives" (Mezirow, 1991, p. 223). *Meaning perspectives* develop during the socialization process in childhood and "refer to the structure of assumptions within which new experience is assimilated and transformed by one's past experience within the process of interpretation" (Mezirow, 1990, p. 2). Meaning perspectives "mirror the way our culture and those individuals responsible for our socialization happen to have defined various situations" (Mezirow, 1991, p. 131). The process of transforming meaning perspectives is referred to as *perspective transformation*, which Mezirow (1991) defines as the process of becoming critically aware of how and why our assumptions have come to constrain the way we perceive, understand, and feel about our world; changing these structures of habitual expectation to make possible a more inclusive, discriminating, and integrative perspective; and finally making choices or otherwise acting on these new understandings. (p. 167)

Transformative learning becomes possible after a *disorienting dilemma* or concern surfaces, triggering critical self-reflection, which in turn creates a change in meaning perspectives, leading to a particular action. A disorienting dilemma could trigger an adult's decision to return to school due to some

Figure 2.1. Artstories RVA: Critical Thinking Through Creativity

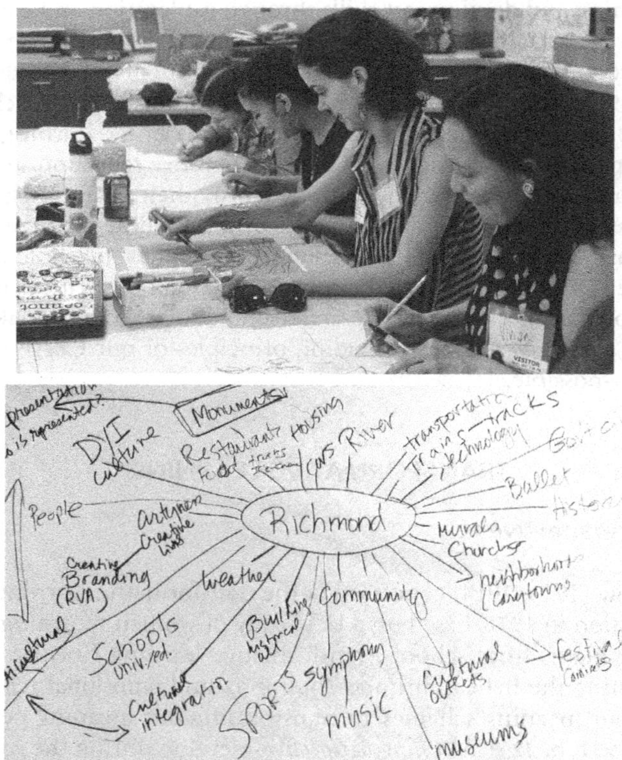

Artstories RVA (2017), an age-integrated arts learning program, took place during after-school hours in the art room of a middle school in Richmond, VA. It provided college students, their professor, two art teachers, and four young teens with an opportunity to collaborate and critically reflect on the Richmond community through artmaking. Stakeholders created word webs on their thoughts and hopes for the Richmond community that were then translated into individual woodcuts printed as one image, unified through physical elements unique to Richmond (railroads and the river). The word webs allowed for critical thinking and connecting to personal experience, making the overall activity both personally and collectively transformative.

dissatisfaction with life or work, and this experience could produce a change in their meaning perspectives. As Mezirow points out, disorienting dilemmas are not necessarily negative, and not every disorienting dilemma leads to transformative learning (Lawton, 2004a).

Lawton's research (2004a) suggests that the story-sharing and creative collaboration generated by CBAE can provide the impetus for an *empowering event* to occur; in this way, CBAE can be a catalyst for critical reflection and self/communal empowerment, and thus for transformational learning. Lawton's research also suggests that transformative learning can occur in adolescents and is not solely an adult theory of education. As described above, the concept of transformative learning connects with all five CBAE E.R.E.C.T. guiding principles: *educational, reciprocal, empowering, collaborative,* and *transformative.*

Sociocultural Models of Transformative Learning

Since Mezirow published his theory of transformative learning, several theorists have criticized and/or expanded upon his ideas. Taylor (2008) divides these theories into three groups or models and seven perspectives. The model that most concerns us here is the *sociocultural,* which includes the social-emancipatory theory of Freire (1970), in which transformation is an unveiling of reality, a process that is ongoing and never-ending. Freire's theory diagrams the social transformation of the oppressed through an awakening of their critical consciousness (educational) that leads to empowerment (empowering). For Freire, the main purpose of transformation is empowerment, and through self-empowerment, society itself is transformed (reciprocal).

Another sociocultural approach to transformative learning, in conjunction with our notions of CBAE, is Tisdell's (2003) cultural-spiritual view of transformative learning. Tisdell's research posits that transformative learning is most likely to occur when an individual is "engaged on three levels of their individual being: the cognitive, the affective, and the symbolic or spiritual" dimensions (Tisdell & Tolliver, 2001, pp. 13–14). This perspective supports Mezirow's view of critical reflection as key to transformation; however, contrary to his relatively basic view of critical reflection through rational discourse, Tisdell and Tolliver (2001) propose that the affective or heart/soul level is equally crucial to transformation: "Transformative learning is perhaps better anchored if we engage on the spiritual level ... and draw on how people construct knowledge through unconscious processes" such as art, creative writing, and story-sharing (p. 14). Below is their definition of spirituality, including the E.R.E.C.T. guiding principles connected to it:

a. A connection to the life force, or higher being or purpose; *transformational*
b. A sense of well-being and interconnectedness of all things; *reciprocal*
c. Meaning making; *collaborative*

   d. Continual identity development, moving toward authenticity;
      empowering
   e. The construction of knowledge through unconscious and symbolic
      processes, like art making; *educational.* (2001, p. 13)

Tisdell and Tolliver (2001) also believe that "for learning to be transformative and culturally relevant, people need to be engaged in learning that pays attention to the sociocultural aspects of their being . . . regarding issues of race, gender, class and culture" (p. 14). Furthermore, these positionalities and intersectionalities "are related to the following intersecting dimensions: the personal, the structural, the cultural, [the historical], the political and the sacred" (Tisdell & Tolliver, 2001, p. 14). The sociocultural model of transformative learning, particularly the social-emancipatory and cultural-spiritual perspectives outlined above, relate to all five of the guiding principles of our CBAE conceptual framework.

CBAE AS ENGAGED PEDAGOGY/ANDRAGOGY

Many of the writings of social activist and author bell hooks (1990, 1994, 1995) speak to the "isms" and phobias that prevent society from moving forward in a more positive and culturally inclusive way. The discriminatory practices of racism, sexism, classism, religion, and gender bias, together with widespread ideological differences, make educational reform a difficult prospect. hooks "proposes an engaged pedagogy to counteract the overwhelming boredom, disinterest, and apathy that so often characterize the way professors and students feel about the teaching and learning experience" (Florence, 1998, p. xvi). An engaged, or reconceptualized, pedagogy is one that engages learners in the educative process because it is relevant to their lives, supports a multicultural and pluralistic society, encourages student empowerment, and links theory to practice in meaningful and intrinsically motivating ways (Florence, 1998; hooks, 1994; Pinar, 1975).

CBAE artist-educators design and deliver curricula that are culturally responsive (Gay, 2010; Ladson-Billings, 2009) to learners' needs and backgrounds (see Figure 2.2). CBAE is engaged pedagogy/andragogy that encourages stakeholders to be *transgressive:* to question and break down barriers, to be self-expressive and self-empowered, and to shift paradigms through collaborative creative endeavor. Methodologically, it inspires all stakeholders to be truth-tellers; and to marshal personal and collective creative expression that, when shared with the broader community, can be both empowering and transformative.

CBAE RESEARCH PARADIGMS

CBAE researchers are most likely to employ interpretive and/or critical theory research paradigms; that is, methodologies that are qualitative, take place in

Figure 2.2. Craft as Empowering Creative Expression

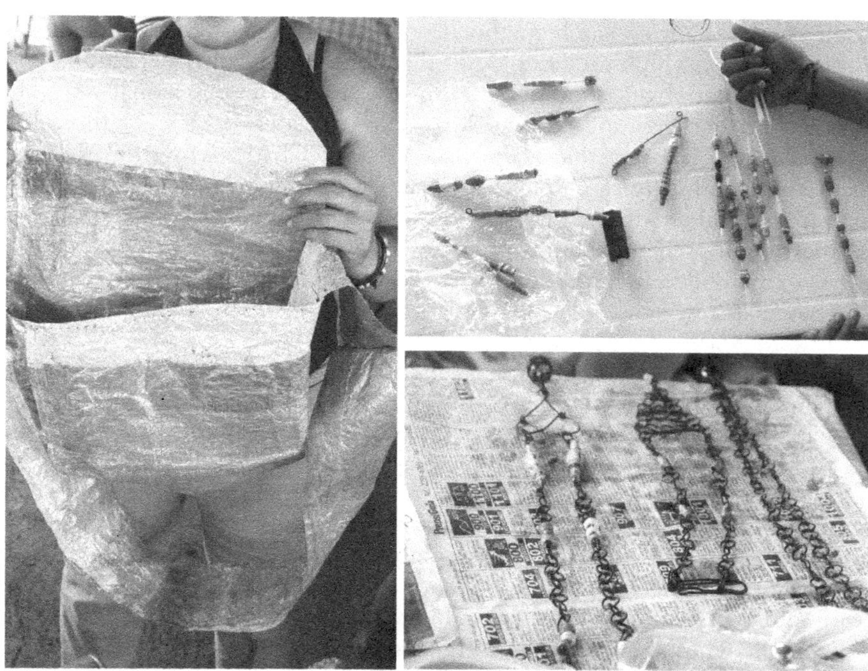

The Nicaragua Project (2011) involved college students working with two trash dump communities— refuse sites where the people who separate trash from recycling are allowed to live, and to build homes, schools, and churches—in Managua, Nicaragua, making craft items from discarded paper, plastic, and scrap metal. Stakeholders collaborated to create jewelry and handbags that the community later sold. Stakeholders, women, and children continued to hone their craft, and with the money they received from sales they developed a cooperative, investing their income in higher-quality materials. To this day they continue to make and sell their craft items. This collaborative partnership led to economic empowerment for the communities and resulted in a healthier lifestyle.

naturalistic settings, are conducive to a humanist perspective, and encompass the researcher's role as participant and observer (Lawton, 2004a). These include critical theory methodologies such as feminist, educational, and social justice and qualitative methodologies such as narrative, ethnography, case study, and phenomenology (Miraglia & Smilan, 2014). Qualitative methodologies rely on thick description and inductive analysis through identification of themes and categories that are interpreted in relation to the questions posed. The resulting themes/categories are then analyzed through a dependable, creditable, and trustworthy conceptual framework that integrates research methods with theory generation to create generalizable knowledge/solutions regarding important questions or problems that communities face.

CBAE Research Methods

Some of the many research methods—or tools specific to a qualitative or critical theory research methodology—that are used to gather data for CBAE research are narrative co-inquiry, life history, arts-based educational research (ABER), a/r/tography, and participatory action research (PAR). For those interested in the learning that takes place through CBAE—as well as the immense potential its research offers for new, generalizable knowledge—a brief description of these methods follows. This overview of research methods is by no means comprehensive but is intended to give the novice CBAE researcher access to methods and frameworks suitable for collaborative, creative, community-based art research.

Narrative Co-inquiry. In many instances CBAE researchers work with vulnerable populations; that is, communities that are constantly researched yet seldom accorded the status and benefits of equal research partners, such as access to (and/or decisionmaking power over) research results and dissemination. Narrative co-inquiry is a collaborative research method carried out *with* rather than *on* people, which accounts for the counternarratives of racial minorities and others, which are so often subordinated by the master narratives that dominate society, educational theory, and practice (Milner, 2013). Narrative inquiry involves "attending to and acting on experience by *co-inquiring with* people who interact in and with classrooms, schools, [communities], or other contexts into living, telling, retelling, and reliving stories of experience" (Huber, Caine, Huber, & Steeves, 2013, p. 213). Narrative inquiry looks at stories as one of the ways in which people create meaning in their lives. People tell stories for a myriad of reasons: to project a sense of self or community, to make sense of complexity, to explore ideas, to celebrate, to salve emotional or psychological wounds, to connect people to community, to inspire people to do good things, to preserve traditions and histories, and to teach younger generations how to live and survive. Story is the unit of analysis in narrative co-inquiry, whose goal is to make meaning through storied examination of lived experience (Clandinin & Connelly, 2000). Most CBAE research includes some aspect of storytelling, visual, written, oral, or performed.

Life History. Like narrative inquiry, life history research is about relationship: the connection that evolves between the researcher(s) and researched as a means of understanding and making meaning from the experiences of others. Building a "good rapport with the person[s] being interviewed facilitates an openness to explore experience and to co-create meaning" (Aston, 2001, p. 145). Life history research "is based on principles of reflexivity, relationality, and artistry" (Cole & Knowles, 2001, p. xiii). Life history can be described as a type or category of narrative (Hatch & Wisniewski, 1995); that is, "life history is always the history of . . . a single life, told from a particular vantage point, while narrative may be a style of telling, a particular way of constructing the story of several individuals or a group" (Lincoln, as cited in Hatch & Wisneiwski, 1995, p. 115). Portraiture, a form of life history research as conceived and documented by Sara Lawrence-Lightfoot, is another narrative inquiry method that may be of interest to CBAE researchers, particularly for its illuminating connections to the field of art education (Lawrence-Lightfoot & Davis, 1997).

Arts-based/arts-informed/arts-based educational research. Barone and Eisner (2011) describe arts-based research (ABR) as a research method that includes both the processes and products of artmaking, whereas Bresler (2014) sees ABR as being primarily about the process, and "the ways in which the arts provide rich and powerful occasions for perception and conceptualization for both audiences and artist, facilitating a dialogue that allows expansion and transformation" (p. 220). ABR views artmaking as meaning-making, a way of knowing and becoming. The artistic product is data, a visual narrative, or a research artifact.

Arts-informed research (AIR) "infuses the processes and forms of the arts into scholarly work" (Cole, Neilsen, Knowles, & Luciani, 2004, p. 9). "In AIR all aspects of the research, from defining the topic, the question(s), and data collection processes to presentation are informed by the arts" (Blaikie, 2014, p. 239), and typify a multidisciplinary model. Blaikie integrated her approach to AIR with Cole and Knowles's (2008) original theoretical framework of the method as follows:

1. AIR corporates research and creation;
2. The researcher and participants are present, thus enhancing validity [dependability];
3. AIR has a moral purpose and a social agenda;
4. AIR work enhances accessibility to research and public engagement; and
5. AIR is transformative educationally and artistically for all participants, including the researcher. (Blaikie, 2014, p. 239)

Pamela's Artstories RVA projects demonstrate all five components of the AIR framework. The project began with a research question, "What would an art-based, age-integrated curriculum theory look like in practice?" The social justice alphabet books created by stakeholders and the artist-educator served to develop empathy and appreciation of difference and as a means of educating multiple generations on the impact of silence on social justice issues that negatively affect people's daily lives, in particular members of the LGBTQ+, Black, and Brown communities.

A/r/tography. This arts-based educational research (ABER) method, conceived of by Irwin and de Cosson (2004), is a living practice "in which knowing, learning, and making" (Triggs, Irwin, & O'Donoghue, 2014, p. 253) are intertwined, and the artist-teacher's identities as artist, educator, and researcher complement one another in a holistic way, allowing for overlap in professional and personal life. A/r/tographers see their art practice as a form of research inquiry (Irwin & de Cosson, 2004; Sullivan, 2010). A/r/tography is a practice-based methodology that deals with the continuity of becoming; it explores the interlocking roles of artist, researcher, and teacher, and how "each [of these] spheres harbor many processes of transition that coexist, co-adapt, and mutually influence one another" (Triggs et al., 2014, p. 258). Many artist-educators involved in CBAE teaching and research embody the tenets of a/r/tography, in that they take a holistic approach to their professional practice, finding ways to integrate their personal art practice with their teaching and research. As a printmaker Pamela has done this with several CBAE projects she has been involved with, such as the Carving Out Freedom project, which involved stakeholders and artist-educators making woodcuts (Pamela's specialty) and teaching a college course as part of the project.

Participatory action research (PAR). Each of the aforementioned research methods encompasses some aspect of PAR. PAR is a collaborative methodology in which the researcher plays an active role with community members to address specific issues or concerns within that community by means of a study (Lawton, 2004a). The data collected by the group are used to plan and shape future action. It is not intended to solve a problem, but rather to understand and improve upon a given situation (Lawton, 2004a). This method is used frequently in educational research—a discipline with strong ties to social, economic, and political justice—in which teachers and the practice of teaching become agents of transformative change and learning (Bresler, 1994). As a research methodology in the field of education, action research is most often used to explore curriculum inquiry and to develop curriculum theories (McKernan, 1996). Participants in an action research study examine their own thinking and practices to effect positive change. Action research is an ongoing, structured spiral process of praxis or reflective action, generating change that moves from initial plan to action, then to reflection, revision, and then further action (Lawton, 2004a; Lewin, 1958; Kemmis & McTaggart, 1988, 1998).

In a participatory action research study, stakeholders and the artist-educator take an active role in identifying the concern and designing a plan of action. Implementation and change are group decisions (May, 1993). This is what makes PAR an ideal research method for CBAE. Action research empowers each individual and decentralizes decision making. It is an inherently democratic process. Both theory and practice are of equal importance in an action research study; each informs the other, and practice is used to validate a theory (Lawton, 2004a). According to Eisner (2006), research as a whole can be conceptualized as "a process intended to enlarge human experience and promote understanding . . . [and] is concerned . . . with the creation of knowledge . . . [and] the process of knowing" (p. 9). Artist-educators involved in action research seek ways of increasing understanding of their own theories, as well as of their educational and artistic practices, through examination of their histories and pedagogical contexts (Bresler, 1994). Lawton's (2004b) CBAE dissertation research was a PAR study that led to the development of her age-integrated arts curriculum theory.

An Age-Integrated Art Learning Curriculum Theory

Lawton's (2004b) dissertation research, *Artstories*, an epistemological action research study of an age-integrated, reciprocal arts learning program, examined learning and social relationships that evolved among three generations of women and girls (previously unknown to one another) who worked together on a collaborative visual and verbal narrative based on their life experiences (Lawton, 2004a).

Artstories is a term conceived by Lawton (2004b) to describe her personal artmaking processes: a combination of visual imagery and verbal text in the form of fine art prints, artist's books, and assemblages that preserve, explore, and reinterpret family/cultural history, identity, and intergenerational relationships. The term was later expanded from the personal and individual to the general and collective. In this context, Artstories describes the process of combining oral, written, visual, and performed narratives into artworks representative of a multiplicity of generational and cultural voices; the issues raised have to do with coming of age within a multicultural society, as well as those common rites of passage associated with being in and passing through the various stages of psychosocial development as defined by Erik Erikson.

An artstory, then, is a conceptual term that can be defined as one's personal quest for identity and meaning through art and story; or, alternatively, as a group's collaborative search for communal, intergenerational, and multicultural understanding through shared oral histories, collaboratively written identity pieces on life themes related to psychosocial development, and visual treatments of these themes created by a group. These artstories are then exhibited, or read/performed for others, as a means of furthering multicultural and communal understanding through artstory sharing. For the stakeholders in artstories, art was used as a means of communicating, and stories as an occasion for artmaking (Christiansen, 1997).

According to Lawton (2004a), artstories was designed to trigger critical self-reflection and sociocultural transformative learning through an *empowering event*, Lawton's (2004b) counter term for Mezirow's (1990) *disorienting dilemma*, the catalyst for critical self-reflection that may lead to transformative learning. Artstories:

- Emulated the creative learning environment of extended family networks.

- Fostered social, moral, and arts learning.
- Generated a sense of community among two or more generations of participants.

The results of this and many other community-based artstories research projects conducted by Lawton over the last 17 years suggest the immeasurable benefits of an age-integrated art curriculum theory. The decline of extended family networks, resulting in legitimate concerns about the social and moral education of children, the isolation of the older adult, and the rise in negative stereotypes and attitudes about adolescence and aging, were the impetus for the first artstories study Pamela conducted. Now more than ever, there is a need for critical intergenerational, multicultural CBAE programs and research to help bridge the gaps of understanding between cultural and ideological differences, and to nurture inclusive sociopolitical practices.

Lawton (2004b) posits an age-integrated arts learning curriculum theory merging three distinct areas that share some kinship via the feminist perspective of relationship-building:

1. A reconceptualist curriculum focus through sharing personal autobiographical narratives;
2. An arts-based empowering event that leads to social transformation (in the Freire/Tisdell sense); and
3. The addition of an intergenerational component to Erikson's stage theory of psychosocial lifespan development.

Based on reconceptualist curriculum ideology, an age-integrated arts learning curriculum theory embraces the autobiographical experiences of the learners, including their artistic interests; the literature, media, and visual culture that influences their perceptions and actions; and the social, political, and moral issues that drive their critical consciousness, all of which inspire them to make connections by way of their art, writing, performance, and personal lived experience to educational institutions and the broader community (Lawton, 2004b).

A reconceptualist curriculum relies on personal, social, and political realities rather than standards, objectives, and lesson plans (Benham, 1979). However, given the standards-driven climate in the United States, we have included ways in which the National Coalition of Core Arts Standards (NCCAS) may be incorporated into school-based CBAE projects (see Appendixes D & E), for those artist-educators required by their school districts to connect their curricula to standards. Reconceptualist curricula are based in autobiographical narrative and are self-directed: the learner is both the center and author of their curriculum. The artist-educator helps to guide the learners' individual curriculum experiences, as well as their awareness of it, feelings about it, and personal interpretations of its meaning (Benham, 1979).

An arts-based curriculum theory embracing age-integrated learning requires restructuring of Eriksonian psychosocial stage theory, as age-integrated learning is tied to his concept of generativity and lifespan development. VanderVen (1999) suggests the addition of the following two sub-phases to address psychosocial development in terms of intergenerational interactions:

Efficacy versus passivity—occurring around age fifty, when investment in the next generation, often exemplified by raising children and serving the community, would remain salient developmental tasks; but may be accompanied by a sense of efficaciousness or instrumentality (i.e., feeling able to have an influence in some endeavor). Some studies suggest that this phase may be an especially vital period in [a caregiver's] development, as energy that was previously expended caring for young children becomes available for tasks outside the home.

Investment versus detachment—involves heightened perceptions of meaning and significance with respect to one's personal belongings and surroundings, as well as to personal relationships. The focus of this phase is not the acquisition of material goods, but an increased appreciation of one's life, with all that it entails. Characteristics associated with this developmental period may intensify gradually as the older person's friends and family members die and a sense of continuity is bolstered by one's attachment to cherished objects and relationships. (pp. 37–38)

In participatory action research, for example, CBAE projects like Artstories—based in shared autobiographical visual, oral, written, and performed co-narrative inquiry—the artist-educator's curricular experiences intersect with those of their learners as they search for a better understanding of their teaching practice, and learners seek to gain deeper cultural, social, and moral understandings. The result is an improvement in the daily practice of teaching and improved understanding of self, other to self, and self to school and community (Conle, 2003).

Conle (2003) writes about narrative moments of encounter, that is, narrative moments characterized by a spontaneous metaphorical connection of one person's life narrative to that of another that they are listening to, observing, or reading—much like the empowering events that flow from creating artstories (community-based art) together. Narrative encounters that produce several spontaneous metaphoric connections (with more than one person at one time, as in CBAE) are "particularly productive curricular events because they facilitate a potential reshaping of one's prior experiences in light of the current encounter" (Conle, 2003, p. 11).

Through age-integrated arts learning, students express and share their personal voices, lived experiences, and social, moral, and political concerns, while erasing barriers between school and community, middle age, old age, and youth. Thus, they inaugurate positive, emancipatory social change that allows them to see and make connections between their classroom learning and life after school (Lawton, 2004b). Listening to the voices of others is an essential means of learning. We connect with, teach, and learn from others by sharing our experiences narratively. These narratives take many forms: oral, written, visual, and performed. Finding an artistic medium in which several of these modes of narrative expression converge to form an art piece or artifact can make our personal thoughts and experiences tangible and resonant to others, even to learners who are quite different from ourselves.

As artist-educators, our greatest challenge is to develop teaching and learning strategies for learners across the lifespan, usually within the school and the surrounding community. Incorporating intergenerational CBAE projects like artstories provides a learning opportunity by way of narrative collaboration with a diverse population, something few students get to experience. As facilitators of learning, our role as artist-educators and researchers is to descry the connecting threads within these narratives and weave them into a common language to be shared and understood by several generations—creating a rich tapestry of people, voices, and images. Collaborative forms of narrative expression can open communication and foster empathy, respect, and understanding across disparate cultures and ideologies, developing what Nussbaum (1997) refers to as "world citizens," people who seek and embrace value in all of humanity (Lawton, 2004b).

SUMMING UP, LOOKING AHEAD

Definitions of CBAE differ across the spectrum of the various community-engaged art practices in use. As artist-educators and researchers, we view CBAE as community-engaged art practices that are concerned primarily with knowing and learning in ways that are personally and socially transformative, building more inclusive communities. The goals of CBAE, as noted in the Introduction, should be a **C.A.L.L.** (*Connect*, collaborate and create through; *Art-based* activities that are community-asset-centered; *Listen* to the stories/voices of others to; *Learn* and build more inclusive and equitable communities and practices) to action. As discussed in Chapter 1, we suggest a conceptual framework comprising five principles—*educational, reciprocal, empowering, collaborative,* and *transformative*—for designing, implementing, and assessing CBAE programs.

Additionally, CBAE embraces stakeholders of all ages from a variety of sociocultural, gender identity, educational, economic, political, spiritual, racial, and ethnic backgrounds. This calls for a holistic understanding of the ways in which people develop cognitively, psychosocially, physically, linguistically, and artistically or creatively. The primary goal of CBAE—as we see it—is learning and making meaningful connections with others through art. An understanding of educational theories connected to the guiding principles of CBAE should greatly assist artist-educators in developing and delivering CBAE curricula that are most appropriate to the stakeholders involved. The educational theories discussed here are just a few of the many possible approaches for designing CBAE programs. For instance, coordination with state standards and the National Coalition of Core Arts Standards (NCCAS) is highly feasible for pre-K–12 artist-educators in private as well as public schools interested in developing CBAE curricula for their students and adhering to standards of learning. For artist-educators interested in conducting CBAE research, several arts-based research methods were presented; many of these methods are still emerging, and more published studies on their efficacy are needed. CBAE research is still a growth industry.

Despite the informal and unstructured nature of CBAE programs, our extensive experience in developing, implementing, and assessing multigenerational CBAE programs has convinced us of the need for an age-integrated arts learning curriculum theory for artist-educators working with older and intergenerational populations.

In Chapter 3, we discuss how the foundational theoretical concepts described above are put into practice.

Getting Started

Locating Stakeholders and Communities

This chapter considers the more specific aspects of CBAE—for example, who should practice it and why. We propose a list of tenets for community engagement while examining the role of CBAE in navigating systems of power and privilege. The chapter closes with suggestions for locating communities to work with.

WHY COMMUNITY-BASED?

Each CBAE project has its origins in some initial motivation. Sometimes it is initiated by a teacher, artist, or community member who is hoping to build connections with others through artmaking. These stakeholders tend to be motivated by many of the principles and goals mentioned in Chapter 1: to provide educational opportunities, to develop connections through reciprocity and collaboration, and/or to create empowering and transformational experiences for all involved. Others might be asked to design a community-based project for a grant, as an assignment in a course, or as part of a professional development institute, hoping to better understand how working closely with a community can be so imperative at this time in our society.

As discussed in Chapter 1, there are many compelling reasons for participating in community-based work, and the arts' role in decentering critical conversations around sensitive sociopolitical issues and systems of oppression is one of them. Everyone has a stake in the health of their community. We suggest observing the following tenets when considering the interests and roles of community stakeholders and the importance of CBAE in establishing common ground.

Work with the Community to Form Connections

When we encourage participants to work together with others outside of their usual circles or purview, they soon begin to recognize kinship where before (it seemed) there were only dissimilarities, and empathy where before there were only misunderstandings (Haedicke, 2016). Identifying shared experiences, interests, and life stories helps banish the idea of the *other*, or the *us versus them* mentality. It also raises the opportunity to celebrate our differences in a positive way. These connections may lead to learning about local artists and art forms, and the wealth of skill and knowledge within other participants' communities (Adejumo, 2000; Fehr, Fehr, & Keifer-Boyd, 20), as well as a deeper understanding of the environment and conditions in which others live (London, 1994). This leads to greater pride in one's own community, together with a new appreciation of the contributions of community members of various backgrounds and skills. When working with a group of music teachers in a rural region of Maryland one summer, Margaret asked the teachers to identify musicians within their local community whom they might collaborate with for a community-based project. They responded that there were none. Finding it hard to believe that there was no folk, improv, jazz, or any other sort of local music scene, she had them do some research in their schools and communities. The number of local musicians they discovered—from students' relatives to the local veterans' and senior homes and elsewhere—surprised the teachers. This led to some enriching collaborations for both the participants and the teachers themselves.

Work with the Community to Encourage Communication

The participatory nature of community-based work opens communication channels between different communities, many of which live side by side but are separated by seemingly insurmountable beliefs, generations, education levels, economics, cultures, or simply neighborhood boundaries (Haedicke, 2016), as well as those who "formerly had no way to express opinions outside their own sphere" (Keifer-Boyd, 2000, p. 156), due to actual or perceived barriers. Many of the misunderstandings between communities are the result of a lack of shared spaces and shared experiences for conversation. When people work together on designing and creating artworks, conversations often turn toward beliefs and life experiences. We have witnessed many instances when participants discover for the first time that many of their experiences and beliefs are shared with the artmakers who are seemingly "different" from themselves. Even more rewarding is seeing individuals consider ideas and points of view that counter their own through these informal conversations with others while making art.

Work with the Community to Extend Learning

CBAE creates opportunities for participants to apply their knowledge and skills, together with the material they have studied in other situations. This benefits themselves, their collaborators, and the wider society. The resultant learning is reciprocal. "Community members and the students are each 'serving' and 'being served' by the other and each is benefiting and learning from the other" (Russell & Hutzel, 2007, p. 8). Learning is extended both by applying their skills in a new way and through individual and group reflection, which are crucial components of success (Taylor & Ballengee-Morris, 2004) for a CBAE collaboration. A group of elementary and middle school students working on a collaborative sculpture installation with community members at a local community center drew on their prior knowledge of engineering, physics, robotics, and instrumental music to create an interactive sculpture that could rotate and play light and music through viewer interactions.

Work with the Community to Seek Relevance

Encouraging students to see the "critical connections between what they encounter outside of class and what they see, do and learn in the art classroom" (Congdon, Blandy, & Bolin, 2001, p. 4) fosters a sense that their school learning is connected to—not separate from—their lives outside of school (Lawton, 2014). For example, when students work with the community, particularly in an intergenerational setting, they often encounter others who have lived experiences that the students have studied in history class, or read about in English class. When students hear first-hand accounts of discrimination, survival during hard times, segregation, uplifting moments in history, and the like, their classroom learning comes to life.

Work with the Community to Develop Pride

By working with and learning from artmakers within the community, we can develop pride in a community's cultural heritage. Learning to see neighbors and other community members working in various styles and mediums as artists helps to replace "a dominant culture's homogenous aesthetic practice by celebrating the vibrant aesthetic energy found within a specific community" (Keifer-Boyd, 2000, p. 156). Culture is localized, not imported, "when participants compare their aesthetic values with a diversity of other cultures" (p. 156) through these interactions. This can lead all participants, including the facilitators, to broaden their definition of art—including *who* is an artist—and expands the realm of possibilities in which artists live and work, and by which they enrich our communities daily.

Work with the Community to Build Understanding

By including a greater variety of disparate voices in the artmaking experience (Daniel & Drew, 2011, p. 38), we develop understanding through validating diversity and contextualism. By working with a diverse range of stakeholders, participants have the opportunity to come to new understandings and revelations about others' lives and experiences within this new context. Working together on a studio project builds trust among participants from different communities through the shared discussions, learning, and conversations that occur throughout the artmaking process between and among stakeholders.

Work with the Community to Promote Social Justice

Community-based/public art projects can involve students in thinking critically about social issues that impact all segments of society, such as environmental issues or empowering the disenfranchised, while meeting traditional art goals. According to Lawton (2010), this is a crucial aspect of community-based art education. A discussion of "freedom" during a community woodblock project raised the awareness of many of the participants to disparities in privilege when the question of lack of freedom was raised. One of the community members chose to contribute to the project by directingg a video of spoken-word segments, with participants talking about when they first experienced freedom, or the lack of it. Some of the students in the group had never considered the idea that they would be denied a simple freedom, such as where to live, because of the color of their skin. Shared stories such as this one, by a woman discussing her mother's time in college, was a moment identified by many in the group as transforming their thinking about power and privilege.

Work with the Community to Express Identity

CBAE curriculum and projects enable stakeholders to creatively express a sense of self, sense of place, sense of community (Anderson & Milbrandt, 2005; Keifer-Boyd, 2000; Lawton, 2014), and resilience in all participants (Kim, 2015). We are also developing strategies for "life-long, self-determined, multi-contextual skills for productive and creative participation in society" (Daniel & Drew, 2011, p. 38). When Lawton designed a collaboration between her university students and a group of adults experiencing homelessness, the focus of the project was on quilting and the lives of the participants who utilized the homeless services at a new Urban Ministry Center (UMC)—each one talking about their life stories and sewing together with others. They and the college students sewed their stories and portraits together into two quilts that then graced the halls of the UMC and the university, sharing their stories within their community and creating a connection with the space.

Work with the Community to Emphasize Art's Role in a Democracy

When we work with community members who engage in "a variety of art practices, such as gardening, embroidery, decorative painting, or pottery, and the diverse people who make them" (Bastos, 2002, p. 71), we orient our understanding toward the intrinsic connections between art and daily life. Recognizing that "traditional and contemporary folk art, local crafts, women's art, vernacular art, popular art, and so on" (Bastos, 2002, p. 71) are a valued part of a community's culture challenges narrowly defined categories of high art and low art, and helps us develop a more unified sense of society. Preparing participants to identify, examine, interpret, and appreciate locally produced art encourages participation in the local community and society at large.

Work with the Community to Build Support for the Arts

When community members participate in positive experiences while working with schools, museums, or art centers, they are likely to become allies when support is needed to maintain or build an art program. Outreach endeavors and exhibitions work to showcase arts programs in hope of maintaining support, and for museums to promote interest in their collections and exhibits (Ulbricht, 2005, p. 8). When the community has a role in the planning and process of an art project, this builds support and enthusiasm for the project, which is evidenced by the time, money, and space contributed by the community to it (Keifer-Boyd, 2000). To paraphrase Eliot Eisner (2002), the arts' position in the community symbolizes to the young what adults believe is important.

Work with the Community to Facilitate Transformation

As previously noted, participation in CBAE can be an *empowering event* (Lawton, 2004b), triggering sociopolitical awareness leading to personal and communal transformation (Lawton, 2010). According to Cranton (1994), "transformative learning occurs when, through critical self-reflection, an individual revises old or develops new assumptions, beliefs, or ways of seeing the world" (p. xii). This transformation may result from working with and getting to know others in a deeper way through the CBAE process. It also might be a result of having access to materials and public exhibition opportunities for the first time or to the realization that others are interested in learning their stories, and working together to share their stories with the broader community (Ulbricht, 2005, p. 8).

NAVIGATING PRIVILEGE

It is likely that one of the partners in the CBAE project will be coming to the partnership from a privileged position. Privilege as a social theory can be thought of as special rights or advantages that one group has over another, often based on race, gender, ethnicity, age, education, or social class, among other factors, which can influence one's sense of belonging or worth in society. Whether this partner represents a school, museum, university, or art center, there are ways of working with others so that both parties feel they have an equal role in the project, despite whichever party provides the bulk of the material resources.

Byron White, the Vice Chancellor for Economic Advancement for the University System of Ohio, writes about the importance of community–university engagements to both sides, as "reciprocity, mutual benefit, and peer relationships are essential to creating truly democratic partnerships between campus and community leaders" (2010, p. 67). He argues that the quality of interpersonal relations—that is, how students, faculty, and administrators interact with community representatives—is the key to achieving democratic partnerships, "particularly where cultural, economic, and educational differences are apparent"(p. 67). White's research has shown that conflicts between the institutions and the community are usually not alleviated by constructive interpersonal relationships alone. When one partner has more financial capital, has "greater professional capacity, controls more resources, and is more politically connected than the community," he or she will need to implement strategies in the initial stages of the CBAE project to address this disparity in privilege and power between the partners (White, 2010, p. 67).

White proposes three fundamental practices for accomplishing this: (1) be transparent, (2) send the right people, and (3) share authority. *Being transparent* means being forthright and honest from the start about why you are seeking a partnership with the particular community. No doubt there are altruistic reasons for your interest in the collaboration, but there are usually other reasons as well, and, as White notes, if you are not up front about what these are, the community will invent its own explanations. Your reasons might be connected with what you hope your students will gain through the partnership; how the project fulfills a grant award; your institution's mission; your professional standing; a course assignment; a lifelong dream of yours, and so on —whatever it is, don't be shy. The more up front and honest you are from the start, the stronger your relationship with the other partner will be.

Though the next suggestion, *send the right people*, is directed more to large institutions than to individuals organizing a CBAE partnership, White (2010) points to the importance of the institutional partner's ability to make decisions and respond to the expectations of the community. If you have to have every decision approved by a higher authority, and have no autonomy in your own project to make decisions, this sends a negative message to the community partner—that is, that this collaboration is perhaps not an important priority for your institution.

Finally, and perhaps most importantly, *share authority*, which means sharing resources, power, and decisionmaking. Asking for input from community members, and then using that information to make decisions without them, is not the same as sharing decisionmaking. As White explains:

> Shared authority exists when real people in power can use it to make final decisions. Shared authority exists when a partner has the certainty—not the hope—that its desires will impact the actions of the other partner. There is a litmus test for telling who holds it in greater abundance: the party that decides how money is spent and how individuals' time is deployed. (White, 2010, p. 73)

It is when both partners have equal say in all of the decisionmaking that a truly democratic community-based art education collaboration is accomplished.

GETTING STARTED

One of the first crucial steps when designing a CBAE project is to identify an interested partner. Establishing the partnership at the outset is critical for ensuring that the community is an equal partner in this collaboration and will have input in everything—from the form of the artmaking all the way to the final exhibition.

Finding a Community Connector and Partners

Finding a *community connector*— a person or group of persons with ties to both the community you seek to work with and institutional partners (schools, colleges, museums, etc.)—is a crucial first step, particularly if you do not have an established relationship with the community you want to work with. The community connector has the best interests of the community at heart, is a trusted member of and/or resource for the community, and is well connected with the institution(s) seeking to engage community partners. For example, Jackie Washington, Coordinator at the Six Points Innovation Center (6PIC), is situated within the Highland Park community in Richmond, VA, but is employed by Storefront for Community Design, a nonprofit partner of the School of the Arts at Virginia Commonwealth University. As a faculty member of VCUarts, Pamela Lawton was able to approach Jackie about the Artstories RVA project. Jackie was then able to connect Pamela with youth and their parents about the project, making a partnership possible.

Generally, those who work with community art projects either live or work in a community (or nearby) with which they would like to partner, or travel to a far-off community where they have a connection, whether it be through family, work, school, or religious affiliation. Whatever the situation, the first step to working with a community is to find a way to talk with the community members. This may be done in a variety of ways, but it is generally advisable to find a community partner that has connections with community members. This may be a local senior center, a shelter for people experiencing homelessness (Lawton, 2010), a government agency servicing the community, a community art center, a local business looking for a mural artist to beautify their façade, or many others—the list is endless.

Consider the type of project you are planning, and seek out partners who suit your project. Melissa was the community connector for our Carving Out Freedom project, a large-scale woodblock project that was a collaboration between the three authors, our students, and community members focusing on the idea of freedom. As director of the ArtReach program, developed by the Corcoran Museum/College of Art + Design, Melissa built trusted relationships with youth and parents in the community through art offerings in the ArtReach studio/exhibition space provided by the Corcoran at the Town Hall Education, Arts, and Recreation Campus (THEARC) in the Anacostia neighborhood of Washington, DC. As faculty members at the Corcoran College of Art + Design and the University of Maryland, respectively, Pamela and Margaret were able to collaborate with Melissa on locating stakeholders and using the ArtReach studio/exhibition space for conducting the project. Melissa recruited local participants to provide input and participate in the artmaking side by side with the college students enrolled in CBAE courses. Margaret and Pamela recruited college students interested in CBAE to participate in the project, the universities offered exhibition space, and through a grant we were able to provide financial resources for the project.

The benefit of partnering with a local organization goes beyond cultural cachet, though having a local connection to vouch for your project will likely help give it local credibility. Partners are also invaluable when recruiting both the input and participation of people in the community. They may help you create and distribute flyers, post about the project on their social media sites, connect with other local organizations, and spread the news about your project through word of mouth. To recruit community members for our project, Melissa created flyers that were available to other community-based organizations housed in the THEARC community center; sent emails; spoke directly with former and current students; contacted other organizations within the center; and suggested that we hold our steamroller printing day in THEARC's parking lot on the same day that they hosted a farmers' market. Without this valuable partnership, our project would not have attracted such a great diversity of participants—from those who shared ideas and/or worked on the designs and cut the wood blocks, to the passersby who stopped to participate on printing day.

Remember that the particular kind of community artist you identify (school-based, community-based, institution-based) will determine whether you decide to seek partnership with an organized community group to realize your project. There are advantages and disadvantages to working with partners—the partner may have a built-in community to work with; they might share the financial burden; and, not least, they will undoubtedly bring different experiences to the table. Sometimes, though, working with partners will also mean going through various administrative hoops and over hurdles, especially when children are involved. We go into further detail on the opportunities and challenges of CBAE work in Chapter 5.

Partnering with Schools

Because of the layers of administrative approval, and the fact that you will be working with children, this partnership may require the most footwork for approval, but *because* you will be working with children, it can be one of the most rewarding experiences, and one with a great impact. It is likely that you will need approval from the principal to partner with a school; whether you approach the principal directly, or go through a staff or faculty member who is interested in the partnership and who will then seek approval from the principal, is up to you, and may be dependent upon the situation. We have found that setting up a meeting with the principal and an interested staff member at the start of the conversation is usually a good strategy, as the principal can then give blanket approval for the project, and you can share the expectations you have from the partnership—for example, are you looking for space? Materials? Help with funding? Recruitment of participants? You and the other adults working on your project may also need to complete fingerprinting and background checks, depending on the school district's policies. Many schools have Before and Aftercare Programs, which often are eager to offer their students an art experience during their block of time, which is a boon to the community artist-educator—there you have a ready-made space, as well as a fairly consistent group of eager participants! If you are simultaneously conducting research, you may need approval from both the principal and an institutional review board (IRB).

Partnering with Institutions, Community Centers, and Community Organizations

Depending on the institution, this may be as simple as finding a staff member who is interested in partnering with you, without the layers of approval sometimes necessary with schools. You may consider contacting a community outreach officer, a recreation program specialist, or an arts coordinator at the institution, center, or organization, and request a meeting about your project. Here you will want to discuss recruitment, the time frame of the project, and the meeting days and times, as well as such things as materials, space needs, project ideas, and exhibition possibilities. Similar to working with a school, your partner may offer you a studio or exhibition space and help with recruitment, and may even have access to materials and funding (though this is less likely). In addition, together you may identify other local businesses or community spaces that may be interested in donating materials or space for your project.

Going It Alone

Not all projects require community organization collaborators, useful as they may be. Individual artists or teachers often elect to work directly with individuals in a community, without partnering with other organizations. If this is your plan, you may want to contact local city council members or the local business association to determine a feasible space for installing your work and learn about the permit process for public works of art. You will then have to design a plan for recruiting community participants, decide where to meet with those interested, and also consider ways of funding (perhaps the community has grant opportunities), while being realistic about the possible limitations of this model—for example, work space, where to store the materials and work in progress, inclement weather interruptions if working outdoors, and so on.

Establishing the Community Connector

No matter which one of the above models you choose, establishing *one person* as the community connector is essential. This may be an art teacher, an employee of a community center or organization, or even a community organizer who does not have a ready group of participants but has strong contacts with community members.

In 2016, Melissa applied for and was awarded government funding from the DC Department of Energy and Environment's Stormwater Solutions grant to engage THEARC's community with their local watershed. The intention of the project was to raise awareness of current ecological issues plaguing local waterways, reconnect residents with a sense of place, activate critical conversations around civic engagement, and foster a communal sense of pride in the local and broader community.

Utilizing the arts as a tool to impact responsible eco-citizenship and augment the environmental education curriculum, Melissa developed a collaboration to offer an arts-based program where community members analyzed and critically addressed the community's concern surrounding the highly polluted creek running through the neighborhood.

The project engaged a broad array of partners, but her primary partner was the Washington Middle School for Girls, a resident partner of THEARC. Working with the school's director and administrative staff, the connectors, they aligned shared goals and outcomes that would mutually benefit the students and the broader community. With collaboration arranged among the school's leadership, Melissa met with the science instructor and identified connections to the school's educational programming. Together they selected in-school opportunities where the project could enhance the science curriculum. In-class dialogue also provided an opportunity to encourage students to participate during out-of-school time (see Figure 3.1). To further engage the school's staff and families, Melissa worked with the middle school's Family Relations Director to set up a series of opportunities to participate after school and at weekend events.

With the primary population set, Melissa then searched out local experts in environmental issues to provide key insights and support. She reached out to faculty and students from George Washington University's biology department and greenhouse to participate in the collaboration. She also contacted knowledgeable staff from local organizations including the Aquatic Resource and Education Center, an environmental and aquaculture center; the National Park Service; and the Anacostia Watershed Society to supply educational

Figure 3.1. The Community Watershed and Stormwater Solutions Project

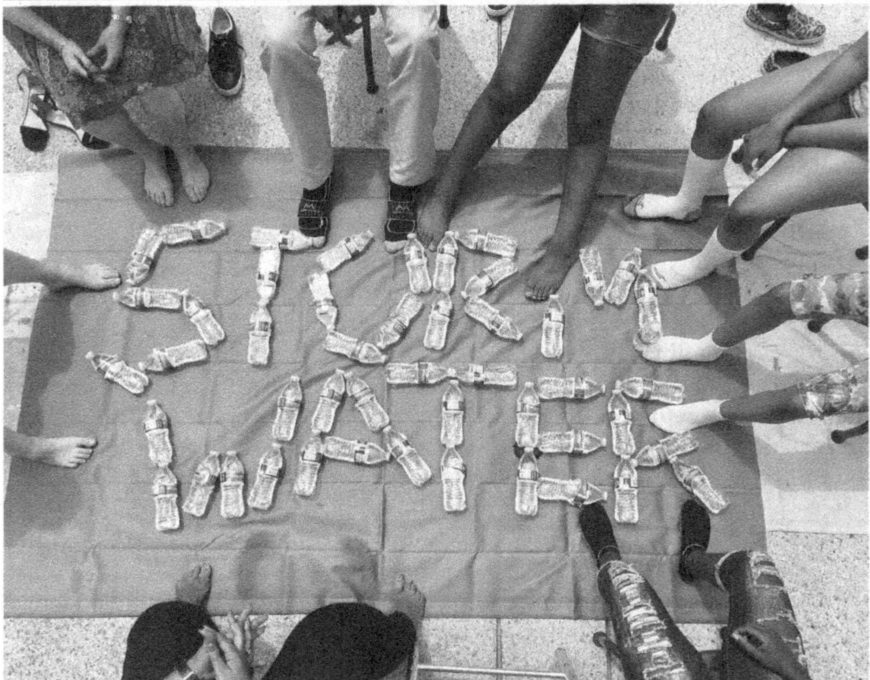

As part of the campaign to reduce litter, participants created a variety of mixed-media artwork after collecting trash polluting the watershed. In response to their experience, stakeholders selected plastic bottles, the most commonly found pollutant, to create a compelling compositional message.

---

support. Each collaborating partner provided a wealth of support, offering hands-on professional and educational assistance, shared resources, and a network of recruiting participation and contagious enthusiasm.

The collaborative project evolved into a shared experience of multiple partners with diverse backgrounds, knowledge, and skills. Each stakeholder worked together toward a clear and common goal, mutually benefitting from reciprocal learning and a shared experience.

Working *with* and *in* the Community

As faculty with limited material resources and funds, and with specific research agendas, it is sometimes difficult to step back from our leadership roles as educators and share autonomy. In community work, sharing power and decisionmaking is what working *with* the community is about. As mentioned in Chapter 1, CBAE is about learning with and through art. CBAE research is about researching *with*, not *on*, the community. The community's voice is key in a CBAE partnership. It may be that only specific materials will be available to you, in which case the suggestion of what might be created with the community may be initiated by you. A theme may even be initiated by you, based on asset-mapping that you have done with the community (see "Mapping the Community's Assets" later in this chapter, and Appendix A). In either case, the community's voice in the decisionmaking process must be heard and considered for a partnership to develop.

Choosing the Project

Once you have identified an interested partner and established the community connector, it is time to work together to choose both the project design and the concept. This is best done through a meeting with all participants—your group of students/artists and the community members. It may be that you have a project in mind, including the topic, the medium, and the space, and are hoping to find community members to work with you to fulfill your vision. This is quite common, and a conventional place to start. On the other end of the spectrum, there are those who are excited by the idea of creating a community-based art project with their participants and are looking to design the project collaboratively. The sections that follow will help you in determining the topic and art form, choosing the time and space, and brainstorming with community members to determine what works best for their community.

Determining the Topic and Art Form. The concept your artmaking will focus around, and the art form the project will take, are ideally determined together as a group. Remember that for community-*based* art projects, you are working *with* a community, which is different from community art projects, which often take place *within* a community. When working *with* a community, community members are given their chance to give input, which is considered in the decisionmaking. If the community is interested in sculptures to beautify a neglected empty space, this may take precedence over the project you had in mind.

Be flexible while considering the practical issues of materials, time, budget, and expertise that you and your group bring to the project, as well as what the community is able to provide. If you hope to create a mural on a three-story building but do not have access to scaffolding, you will not get much further than the ground floor. Whether you have a project in mind or decide to work with the community to develop the project, gathering input from the community is an essential step early on in your planning. This can be done through social media, holding planning meetings in the community in person, and distributing surveys in both paper and digital form. If you have a community partner, ask if they can host a public meeting. Be sure to include various questions in these brainstorming sessions or surveys that will cover necessary topics for input. For logistics on gathering this important feedback, see "Surveying Community Members and Brainstorming Sessions" below.

Finding a Suitable Space and Time for Artmaking. Choosing the studio space is, of course, dependent on the art form you will be using—which is best determined with community input—but lining up available space at the start is advisable. You or your partner may have a studio space if you work at a school or community center, but if not, work together to find a space that is easily accessible to all participants at the times you will be working. You can always change the location if the group decides on a project that is best built on site. A local school's art room may be an ideal setting for designing and working on a mosaic project, but perhaps not for a large sculpture or, of course, a site-specific mural.

Your partner will also know when their constituents are available for a meeting. This can be the tricky part—finding times that work for your group, the community members, the studio space, and you! In our printmaking project Carving Out Freedom, we scheduled our meeting days and times to fit the schedules of our group of working teachers, based on the knowledge that the community members were most available on Tuesdays and Thursdays between school hours and dinnertime. This was based on Melissa's experience working with the community over the years. We also had to consider what times the studio space was available, and, because of the large size of our woodblocks, the feasibility of leaving our materials in the space. And finally, because this partnership was being taught as a graduate class, Pamela and Margaret had to ensure that it fit into the academic calendar as well as the time requirements for the universities—so many pieces to puzzle together! But flexibility and creative maneuvering on the parts of all were what allowed for success. Most importantly, don't forget that gathering input from the community is an essential step in choosing the space and time for your project.

Surveying Community Members and Organizing Brainstorming Sessions. Now is the time to consider what each participant brings to the project: for example, topics of interest for participants; the possible needs of the community; personal knowledge of artists who work in the community and who might be interested in participating; and the artmaking experiences and expertise of all participants. Referring back to our C.A.L.L. to action, brainstorming questions should focus on the following:

- What topics that are current in the community would they like to explore through artmaking? They may be interested in exploring deep social justice issues, such as gentrification or service inequities; or they might be more interested in the celebration of a milestone, local celebrity, or theme of unity—these topics are equally valid, and ideally the voice of the community should guide the idea.

- What are the needs of the community? Are there blighted or unsafe areas that the community would like to focus on to make their community a safer or more beautiful space? Although a tunnel underpass covered in graffiti may not be as visible as a wall in a local shopping center, this may be a space the community would like to reclaim through an art project.
- Who are the local artists in the community who might be interested in participating and sharing their expertise? Every community has artists living among them, and inviting them to share their work and experience with others builds authentic collaborations.
- What are the best times for community participation? In some communities, weekends work best for most, whereas in others certain weeknights may be more open—if you learn this beforehand, you will have a greater chance of a strong turnout.
- What space is accessible and available? When searching for the artmaking space, the community can be an invaluable resource for identifying spaces that are accessible. The local community center might be the obvious choice, but you may have more time flexibility with such spaces as a large recreation room in an apartment building—something the community members might identify in your survey. An added bonus to this sort of space is that it is easily accessible for the residents, which may increase participation rates.

This is where your community partner contact is essential. They are the bridge between you and the community members, and will likely have a good idea about the best way of advertising to recruit community participants. Depending on the project, you may find it valuable to hang flyers in local businesses, or distribute them at the neighborhood schools and centers, and post the information on a community listserv and social media sites. Where and when you will meet together as a group to brainstorm ideas for the project should be decided between you and your partner—you may want to build it into the first day of the established studio time, or set up brainstorming sessions beforehand.

Mapping the Community's Assets. A useful way to gather community feedback is through asset-mapping (see Appendix A). This is a process used in community development to create a map of what is valuable in a community. If we think of the term *asset* to mean "an item of value owned; a quality, condition, or entity that serves as an advantage, support, resource or source of strength" (Dorfman, 1998, p. iii), we can see that communities contain many assets that could be useful for your partnership—spaces, artists, builders, organizers, and so on. In her work with abandoned girls at Casa Hogar, Pamela and her students worked with the girls to create artworks about their experience at the home; this included community assets (local people) and in-kind donations to make a better life for the girls (see Figure 3.2). Dorfman (1998) recommends, in her useful guide *Mapping Community Assets Workbook* (which can be found online), a process for determining the assets each individual brings to the partnership, as well as the assets in the *community where you are working*. Once you have listed the assets, a pool of resources, skills, and knowledge can be defined, and a process of building, creating, and developing your community-based art education project can begin.

Figure 3.2. Choosing a Project with a Community: Showcasing the Home for Girls and the Opportunities It Provides

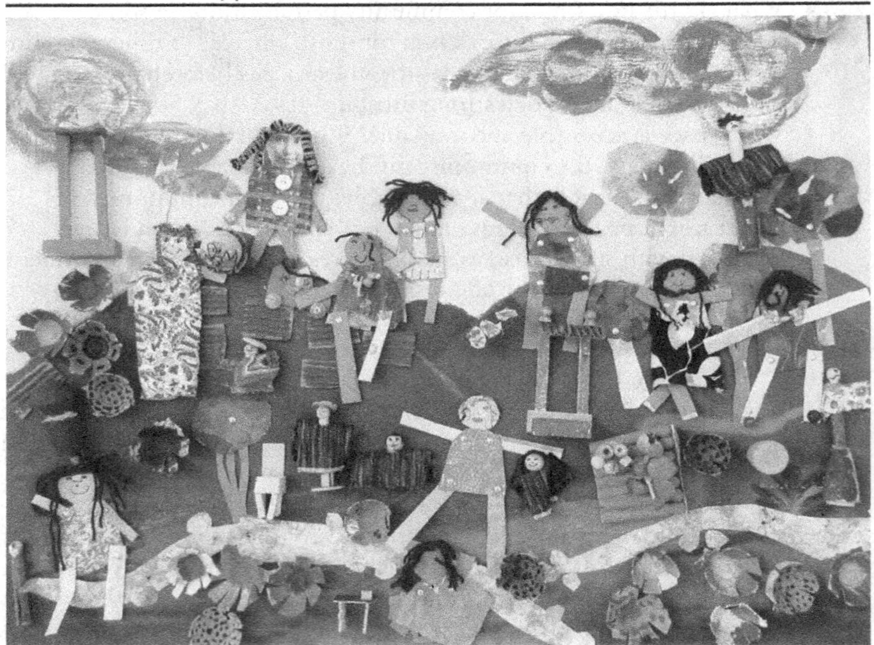

Lawton's social justice art education course in San Miguel de Allende, Mexico, connected with Casa Hogar, a home for abandoned girls aged 3–19. The director was interested in artwork that showcased the home and the opportunities it provided to the girls. She wanted something that would visually tell the story of the home, was portable, and could be used to solicit donations from individuals and charities. With this in mind and using the materials available to them, Lawton's class worked with the girls to create a three-dimensional triptych of life at the home. The director took the artwork to donation solicitation meetings and was successful in receiving in-kind donations and equipment, such as a refurbished kitchen and cooking lessons provided by a local chef. Lawton's students were able to teach art techniques and help the community to meet a need it expressed. This project chosen with the community examined the assets, needs, and interests of all stakeholders.

SUMMING UP, LOOKING AHEAD

You are now at the point where you have found your partner; connected with and learned from the community; decided on the type of community-based project you will undertake; and listed the community's assets. Now is the time to get the planning under way. You may use the checklist below to assist with your planning:

Checklist for Working with Stakeholders and the Community

Find partners in the community
Get the word out
  ✓ Community resources
  ✓ Social media
  ✓ Local flyers
Gather community input through surveys/community meeting
  ✓ Choose the topic and art form
  ✓ Determine the needs/interests of the community
  ✓ Find local resources
  ✓ Ensure community accessibility
  ✓ Determine community members' availability
Map community assets
  ✓ What assets do you and your partners bring to the project?
  ✓ What assets are available in the community?

The ideas discussed here are intended as a baseline for planning and implementing a CBAE project *with* the community. We have found it impossible to plan for every possible scenario ahead of time. CBAE work is unpredictable—unlike teaching from a set curriculum in a formal classroom space, CBAE is informal, and flexibility needs to be built into the design. This uncertainty, like the process of creating a work of art, is where the learning and fun come in. We have learned a lot about the rewards of CBAE work. In Chapter 4, we discuss the planning process and goal-setting.

Planning the Project
Setting Goals and Learning Outcomes

To understand the importance of community input, imagine that you have lived in your home all or most of your life. There are things about your house that perhaps others—and maybe even you—think could be updated or improved, but it is your home and you are comfortable there. Now imagine that a group from a nearby university comes by your house one day and starts to alter your house and yard, with no discussion or feedback from you! They decide your shutters would look beautiful painted purple, or they proceed to install a koi pond in your front lawn, as you stand there gaping at their discourtesy. It is hard to imagine such a thing really happening—and yet it happens with regularity when the community is not fully involved in the planning process for an art project. A case in point is the 1981 community mural in Queens, NY, titled *Martin Luther King: Remembering and Renewing the Dream*. The artist, G. Joe Stephenson, recalls in the book *Walls of Heritage, Walls of Pride: African American Murals* (Prigoff & Dunitz, 2000) having to rework the mural that was in progress, based on community demands. The final image is one of Dr. King in various moments in his life—speaking at the March on Washington, leading a protest, and embracing his family—but this is not what Stephenson had initially planned:

> The only thing that remains is Dr. King with his fist up. There were images of people marching, buses burning, crosses and the KKK, and lots of flames—it really looked dynamic. But some of the people in the neighborhood had a protest. We had to stop work and meet again with the community. They wanted more positive images. I had to go back and research family life. One woman said, "You wouldn't go painting swastikas in a Jewish neighborhood, or scenes of the Holocaust. That's what the KKK means to us." They said they didn't want their kids to see that kind of stuff. It was a learning experience for me as a muralist . . . you can't just do what you want. You're working with people. So, I went back and redesigned it, and this was the result. They liked it. It's tamer than it was. (Stephenson, cited in Prigoff & Dunitz, 2000, p. 136)

When we enter into a community with a goal of *bringing them art*, *giving them a voice*, or *beautifying their neighborhood*, we are neglecting the *core tenet* of CBAE, and that is the participation and input of the community. Whether the idea is in its earliest stage or at the stage where you have received funding, materials, and an offer for an installation space, *participation*, *input*, and *feedback* are vital pieces of the community art puzzle. Keep this in mind as you move forward, and be sure that each of the following steps—developing time limits, a budget, and goals—is done collaboratively with your community partner.

WORKING WITHIN TIME CONSTRAINTS

It is the rare project in which time and money are not an object—if that is your case, lucky you! For the rest, you will be working within a time frame and budget, so these should be at the forefront of your planning, as they will determine the scope of your final project. Remember to account for how many hours you will be meeting as a group for planning and studio work, and be realistic about whether or not work will be done outside of the work sessions. Once you and your community partner establish a time frame, you can make more realistic decisions about the size of the project, and how to organize the studio and planning sessions to ensure that you can complete the project by the end date.

When Margaret joined forces with an art professor at another university to create a community mural, as a step toward unifying the two campuses after a tragedy, they had 3 weeks from the start of classes until the 5-foot-by-16-foot mural would be painted by the community at an arts festival. Their classes overlapped only once a week for 2 hours, which gave them 6 synchronous hours with 18 students—whose campuses were 12 miles apart—to discuss, design, and sketch the drawing on canvas. Over the first 2 weeks, the students met during class time through video conferencing to brainstorm themes and compositions together, and used social media groups in and out of class to share sketches, images, quotes, and influential artists.

The third session was held on Margaret's campus, where both groups of students met together to sketch the design onto the canvas to be painted. It was a tight time frame, but because the artist-educators were realistic during the planning meetings about how much time the students were likely to put into the design outside of class (not a lot), and because they collaborated with the set design program in the performing arts department to prepare the room and canvas for community painting, they were able to accomplish their goal in the time allotted. In addition, they added a final session to meet together after the community painting nights to finalize and unify the mural. This is an important part of the process to keep in mind, especially if working with volunteer community members, as you would all like a finished product that you are proud of, and that is ready for exhibition.

Figure 4.1. Students Meet during Class Time Through Video Conferencing to Work within Time and Space Constraints

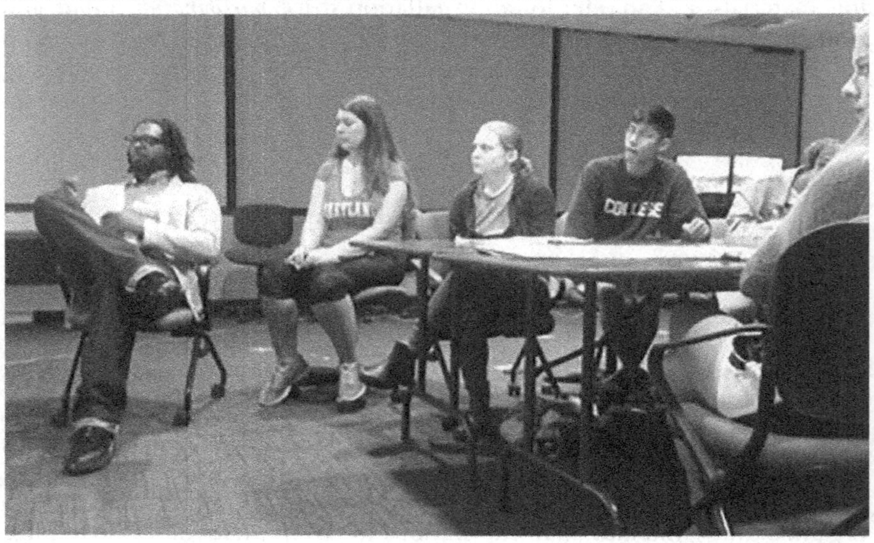

Figure 4.2. Finished Community Mural Meant to Unify Two Campuses after a Tragedy

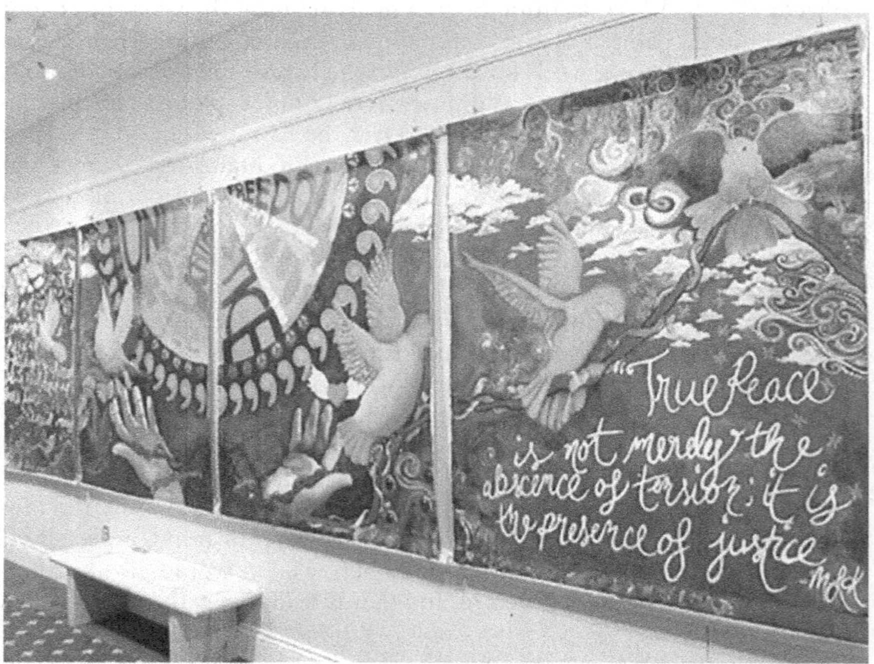

DEVELOPING A BUDGET

Developing a budget with your community partner is the next step in planning. You may already have funding from a grant or another source. If this is the case, you have a set monetary amount to determine the cost of the project, which may include some or all of the following: cost of space (if any), artmaking materials; copying cost for flyers, handouts, and so on; and honorariums for guest speakers, costs related to installation (frames, wires, etc.), and a celebratory reception, if applicable.

If you are looking for funding for the project, we recommend searching for community grants through your state or county arts council and professional development and community engagement grants for college faculty, in addition to fundraising in person or online, and contacting local organizations for in-kind or cash donations. Art materials are sometimes donated by large art stores for community projects, with the promise that you will advertise their generosity, and some nationwide chain stores (e.g., Target) offer grants for schools or community projects—this is how our Carving Out Freedom project was funded.

Finally, when procuring materials, keep in mind all of the possible materials and supplies you might need for the large community work you are creating. For the Carving Out Freedom project, our needs went well beyond the 4' x 8' woodblocks, carving tools, ink, paper, and brayers. We also needed materials for preliminary block-printing work (small linoleum and maple blocks, scratch art sheets, and styluses); spray bottles to dampen print paper; blankets to protect prints from the steamroller drum; wood to construct a jig to hold the various pieces composing each woodblock for printing; rags, solvents, and so forth. Hopefully, you or a collaborator will have worked with the materials or process in the past and will be familiar with what is needed.

We also suggest you add a fund to your budget for last-minute materials. Make a list of what you know you will need, what you think you will need, and materials you don't need but would be great to have if the budget allows. For the Carving Out Freedom project, this included four Dremel rotary tools to help with the carving, which proved quite handy when the public printing day was 24 hours away.

SETTING GOALS AND LEARNING OUTCOMES: SCOPE AND SEQUENCE

Limiting the scope of the project is often one of the hardest parts of the designing process. The desire to make this project the biggest and most impactful experience is understandable and tempting—after all, if it's going to be a transformational experience, why not address multiple issues all at once? The advantage of choosing one focused goal is that the participants can then engage deeply with the idea and the process, as well as complete the project within the time frame.

Idea/Theme Generation

Some projects start with the idea or theme, and the collaboration follows naturally from there. The theme might be connected with a call for artwork, a connection to an artist or project, a topic of current interest, or a recent event. This was the case with Margaret's mural project: a tragedy involving students from both campuses prompted faculty at each institution to consider how they might engage in the difficult and deliberate process of bridging the divides in their community and opening new lines of communication and dialogue. This was the theme that spurred the collaborative art piece.

Other projects begin with the collaboration itself, and the theme or idea is generated once the partners meet. In these cases, the theme of the art project emerges through discussions with the community partner about shared interests or community needs. Perhaps the community is interested in focusing on their neighborhood's history, or would like to celebrate local volunteers, or focus on providing a positive message for their youth to strive for. Together you will find a way to choose the topic on which to focus the artmaking.

Focusing the Idea/Theme for Artmaking

At this point, you either have a concentrated topic and are ready to start the artmaking, or have a very broad topic that needs to be narrowed down in order for the artists to have a focus and to unify the imagery. Each artist has their own way of narrowing down their idea, but when working with groups, we have found the most success by starting with a big idea, then formulating essential questions that the group responds to visually. A *big idea* is a broad topic/concept that students and artists use to make connections among cultures, art and artists, and other subject areas that provides a conceptual focus for understanding our world (Walker, 2001, p. 3). When working with a group, this issue or big idea should be of meaningful interest for all participants to explore. If this is an unfamiliar topic for you, we recommend the many published works of Sydney Walker, Melanie Buffington, and Olivia Gude—as well as the online PBS series *Art 21: Art in the 21st Century*—for examples of how to use big ideas as a catalyst for creative, authentic, and original artmaking (e.g., Buffington, 2007, 2014; Gude, 2004, 2007, 2010; Walker, 2004).

In some instances, the big idea emerges from discussions with the participants, as was the case with Margaret's mural project; through discussions and brainstorming, and debates about what the objective of the project was, they arrived at the concept of *unity* as their big idea. Other times, the artist-educators facilitating the project already have a topic in mind that they are hoping to explore with the community. This was the case with Carving Out Freedom—we were interested in the idea of freedom and what this meant to the various participants. It was a current topic in the news and an important one for guiding participants in discovering new perspectives and understandings.

Guiding Questions

Once a topic is chosen, designing questions to guide discussion and visual imagery development is an essential step toward ensuring that all participants feel comfortable contributing to the design of the artwork. These questions should be "open-ended, provocative, and generative; their aim is to stimulate thought, to provoke inquiry, and to spark more questions" (McTighe, 2004, p. 21). Participants are able to think more deeply about the topic when considering these questions, and to have more open and frank conversations with others—and may even be inspired to do some research on the topic. When working with the topic *freedom* for the woodblock collaboration, we designed questions such as *What is freedom? What does freedom mean to you? What is a time when you felt most free? What is a time when you did not feel free?*

Visual journaling is a useful process for reflection and planning, trying out different visual ideas and collecting images, quotes, and other artifacts that may be used in the planning. If participants are assigned to read articles or do research for the project, the journal becomes a space of reflection. They might add quotes connected with the topic, as well as sketches, images, news articles, or anything else that will guide their artmaking decisions (see Figure 4.3).

The Envisioning Process: Translating Ideas from Words to Images

Creating original and meaningful imagery based on a topic is difficult for many, and if not well guided can result in clichéd (and copyrighted) images, such as hearts, characters from popular culture, and people holding hands. The guiding questions are an important step for the participants to generate ideas for images that speak to their personal connections with the topic, and not just ones they have seen used by others. Margaret was teaching art in New York City when the World Trade Center was attacked on September 11, 2001. Throughout the following semester, the students' artwork was filled with images of U.S. flags, bald eagles, and the Statue of Liberty—these images were ubiquitous on television, newspapers, billboards, and t-shirts, and thus were in the forefront of the students' minds. It was only through regular discussions—using questions designed to encourage the artists to explore their own experiences and feelings connected to the event—that more nuanced and original images began to emerge in their artmaking.

To guide students in this process, making word webs is a useful way to move from ideas to words, and on to images. This is best done as a full-group activity once the participants have reflected on the guiding questions individually or

Figure 4.3. Student Visual Research Journal on Brainstorming Community

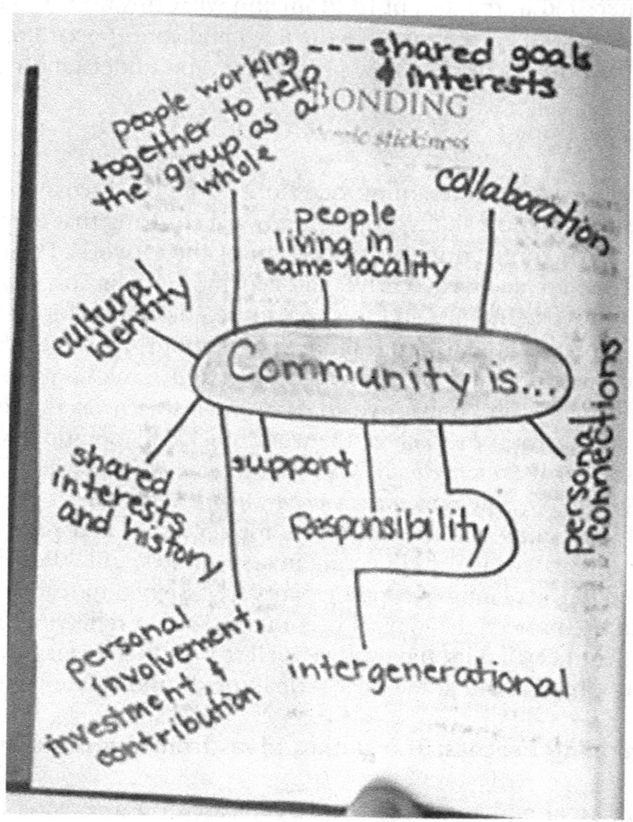

in small groups. To connect their ideas to images, begin with the topic in the center of the board, then branch out to link to words or phrases generated by the group. Each of these is then linked further out to other words or phrases, and finally to images associated with the responses (see Figure 4.4). In the Carving Out Freedom project we explored the topic of freedom. The group created four different word webs, one from each of the guiding questions. For example, participants responded to the prompt *What is freedom?* with words such as *expression, choice, values,* and *struggle.* Once we gathered 20 or so responses that all linked back to our topic, we then organized the responses into three categories that emerged from the responses (see Figure 4.5). The participants then chose their group based on the word list they wanted to work from.

At this point, the participants met in their smaller groups with their word lists, discussed the words in relation to the guiding questions, and began to visualize images that represented the words. This step is the essential bridge between the idea and the artmaking— it ensures that the visual expression speaks to their personal connections. We call this the *envisioning process.*

Figure 4.4. Participants Move from Ideas to Words—Responses to the Prompt *What Is Freedom?*

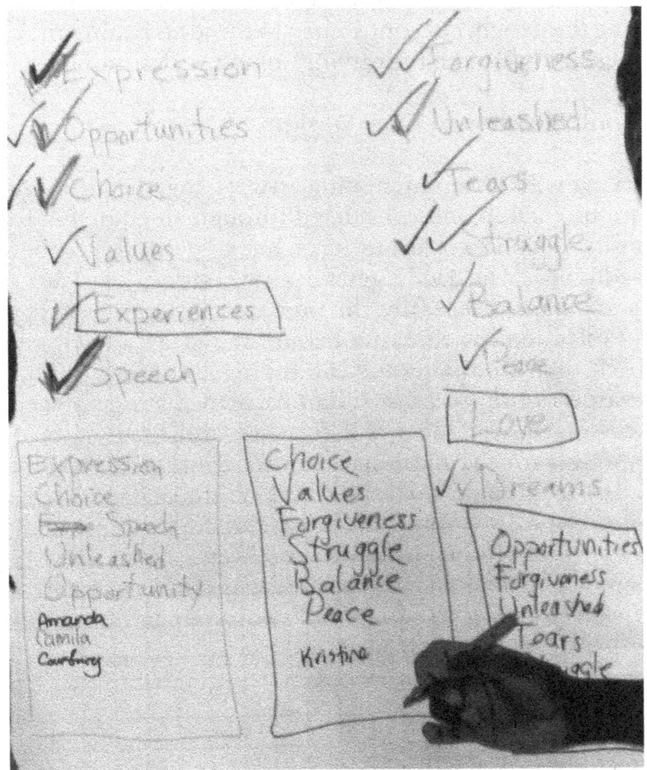

Building Material and Process Knowledge

Often the materials and process your group works with will be unfamiliar to many of the participants. You do want to be sure that all members are comfortable working on the project, whatever their past experience with artmaking. It is often helpful to start the studio work with smaller projects, to help participants gain confidence in the process. If you will be working with carving print blocks for the final piece, for example, you might start with small sheets of scratchboard and styluses (see Figure 4.5), so the artists have a sense of how each mark they make—whether intentional or not—will become a part of the work. Taking some time with the group to explore the material they will use will help ease the uncertainty of some, while serving to familiarize them all with nuances of the material that they might have missed if not given step-by-step instruction. This is a good time to introduce the work of artists who practice in this medium or process in interesting ways to express a big idea. If you have the time and participants are interested, you may assign simple activities for skill-building in a particular medium, but keep in mind that each participant will bring different strengths to the project. When working on our woodblock prints, for example, some of the participants were not comfortable with drawing the design, but contributed to the ideas behind the composition, and were eager to help with the carving, inking, and printing.

Moving from Sketches to Final Design

When working with groups designing artwork together, it is important that all ideas are listened to and considered through an equitable feedback process. This can be done in various ways, but in general, it is best guided by the artist-educator, who facilitates the conversation to ensure equal input from all participants. Generally, the process follows a combination of sharing ideas, explaining the thinking behind the ideas, allowing the group to give feedback, then modifying and combining ideas, with feedback again. An important aspect of this process is that participants reserve their judgments when discussing others' ideas and sketches, and focus instead on neutral questions, to discern the meaning behind others' contributions. For example, instead of making the comment, "I don't understand what the vine has to do with the topic," one could ask, "Please talk to us about your idea behind including the vine." This open dialogue builds trust, and allows for deep conversations in which an atmosphere of mutual respect can develop. Through this discussion process, the group will choose some ideas and images and

Figure 4.5 Participant Visual Journal with Scratchboard Image

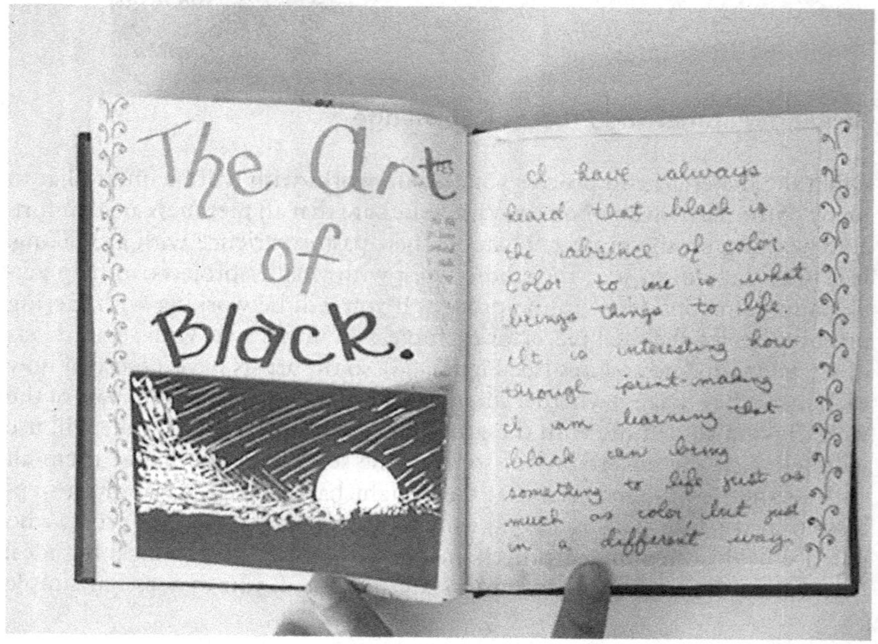

Figure 4.6. Participants Working Together Contemplating Final Sketch for Woodblock

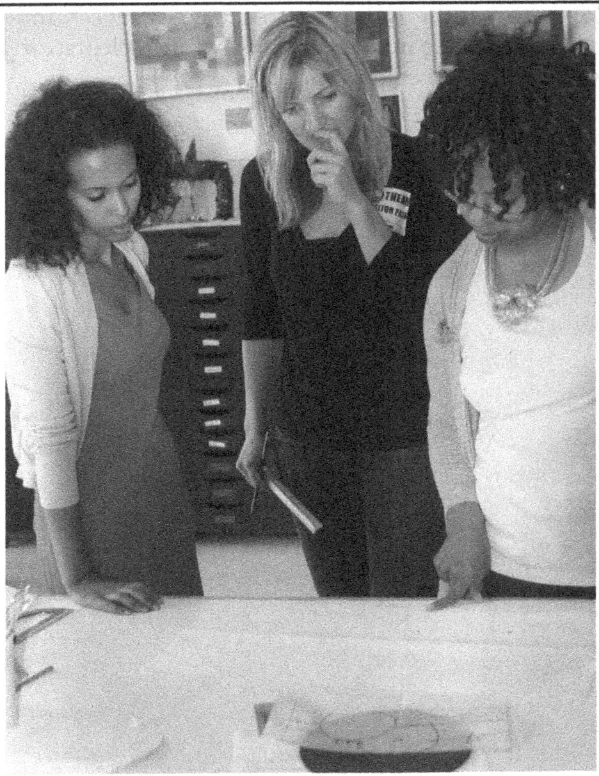

eliminate others, all the while checking in with all group members to be sure they are all in agreement.

When this process is completed, the group should wind up with a strong visual design that all participants are comfortable with and that is ready to guide the final version. When creating the final collaborative piece (or pieces, if they are crafted individually but displayed together as a body of related work) every group member should have the chance to contribute as much or little as they see fit. You will often find that participants who were wary at the beginning about contributing to the artmaking are now invested in the process and eager to literally have a hand in the final piece (Figure 4.6), so be certain to encourage all to contribute, despite initial uncertainties.

SUMMING UP, LOOKING AHEAD

Finally! You have chosen the topic, worked through ideas, sketched various compositions, and are working on the final piece. This is the moment you have all been preparing for, and the hard work that went into the planning and brainstorming is finally paying off. Despite the challenges that you've encountered along the way, this is the moment to enjoy, reflect, and—soon—celebrate! It is now time to dive in to the artmaking, and celebrate together as you exhibit the work within the community.

Part II

IMPLEMENTING, CELEBRATING, AND EVALUATING CBAE PROJECTS

Part II consists of three chapters that move beyond the planning stages of CBAE. Chapter 5 discusses the challenges and opportunities that CBAE projects present, with examples from our own CBAE practice. This chapter is intended to prepare the reader about to embark on a CBAE project with insights into what they may encounter, and how to manage challenges and optimize opportunities. Chapter 6 outlines the importance of celebrating the completion of a project; how planning for celebrating and sharing the results needs to be part of the initial planning process; and, lastly, how events and exhibitions connect to a broader audience and provide opportunities to generate community and creative leadership development. Finally, Chapter 7 presents an overview of processes for assessing learning outcomes and enduring understandings developed at the start of a project, and for sharing this data with all stakeholders. Effective documentation, forms of stakeholder and participant feedback, and obtaining firsthand accounts of what was valued most, what was learned, and what should be changed are all important information for planning and implementing future CBAE projects.

CHAPTER 5

Challenges and Opportunities
Fostering Transformative Experiences

Community-based expressive projects are developed to provide participants with the opportunity to engage within their own communities or explore new ones. They have the ability to reach people and have a meaningful impact on their lives. Community members are not only learning and honing their skills as artists; they are also discovering the transformative power of the arts to access social consciousness and bring about social change.

Community arts enhance the well-being of individuals as well as the public health of communities. Collaborative art projects foster creative expression, promote social connectedness, provide joy and inspiration, provoke relevant dialogue, and involve community participation. By building collective capacity and fostering dialogue, the projects not only beautify spaces but, through engagement, reconnect and transform relationship to place, reduce stigma, encourage empathy, and strengthen the social fabric of the community. Providing personal growth and public education, the art projects can shed light on challenges, offer opportunities to build resiliency skills, and become active agents of progressive social change. Through a collaborative inquiry and art-making process, community projects can be instrumental in increasing self-expression, developing new creative skills, increasing self-efficacy and social identity, enhancing interpersonal skills, promoting greater civic engagement, and strengthening social capital (Matarasso, 1997).

Impactful projects often delve into relevant topics, explore and articulate community issues of concern, or highlight community assets, yet no two CBAE projects are the same. Each is complex, involving specific populations, resources, and goals. While most aim to help reconnect communities and encourage social responsibility, the pathways to getting there and the outcomes can vary vastly from project to project. The common ground lies in creating safe spaces that foster expression, inclusive participation, and democratic decisionmaking that can benefit all those involved.

CBAE projects provide both personal and community experiences with opportunities and challenges. At their best, they offer opportunities to build strong relationships and greater understanding of different cultures, raise public awareness of common community issues, increase a sense of place, and enhance the perception of artmaking. At their most challenging, they must overcome logistical and communication obstacles and move beyond actual or perceived biases and barriers.

There is no secret formula or ingredient to plan or carry out the project, but the processes used are as important as the project itself. Creating art collaboratively requires honest dialogue, mutual respect, and trust. Strong project designs foster learning about one's self while also learning from others. Transformative learning at its best occurs if projects strive to collectively express powerful personal and community stories, open a space for critical thinking and problem solving, provide a public platform for expression, find common ground, and seek to provide an enriching process for all.

Most importantly, projects should strive to answer the essential question: How does the experience meaningfully impact the community? From curriculum design, redesign, and implementation, through installation, celebration, and reflection, the question should be revisited throughout the project.

EXAMPLES OF OPPORTUNITIES AND CHALLENGES IN CBAE PROJECTS

In this chapter, we will discuss the cultural implications often found within CBAE projects, and the many challenges and opportunities you may encounter as you begin to work with community partners. We will highlight the benefits creative collaboration can present for the community, the artist-educator, and society at large. We will also dive deeper into the process of building strong partnerships and enhancing rapport with community members, while designing projects that keep community input and identity at their core, embrace inclusivity, and foster safe, brave, nonthreatening environments that promote open dialogue and expressive opportunities.

To further illustrate the challenges, opportunities, and cultural implications discussed, we begin by discussing two CBAE projects that were led by Melissa as Director of ArtReach at THEARC, a community arts program that provides special arts opportunities for communities in the District of Columbia's Wards 7 and 8, two historically underserved segments of the U.S. capital.

The first, the Community Portrait Project, involved a large-scale collaboration that brought together a variety of participants—Ward 7 and 8 community members, students (ages 8–18) attending ArtReach after-school classes, photojournalism students from George Washington University (GWU), and alumni from GWU's Corcoran College of Art + Design—to create portraits that highlighted the work, inspiration, and impact of eight community influencers. In the second example, Garden Murals, Melissa worked with residents at an apartment complex reserved for young men and women who recently aged out of the city's foster care program, and created four portrait murals for the complex's garden area that were meant to reflect individual residents' identities, relationships to food, and aspirations for the future.

As you will see, each project was carried out differently, with each containing its own opportunities and challenges but always centered on ideas of community identity, inclusivity, and open dialogue.

The Community Portrait Project: Building Collective Efficacy Through Asset-Based Programming

In the fall of 2016, Melissa led a Community Portrait Project, highlighting the assets of Ward 7 and 8 communities in Washington, DC. The project celebrated eight remarkable people through the lens of ArtReach students (ages 8–18), photojournalism students from GWU, and mixed media alumni artists from the Corcoran College of Art + Design. Using a variety of media, the artwork examined stories of the eight individuals who were deemed community influencers and explored their passion, energy, and commitment to the community.

The broad purpose of the project was to introduce and connect community members, raise public awareness and social consciousness of local identity, uplift the community's self-image, nourish and enrich social capital, share intergenerational stories, and celebrate active and engaged citizenship. The process involved interviewing and photographing the eight influencers; holding group discussions, with reflections by students; and mixed-media collaborative portrait-making over three stages of collaboration.

In the initial curricula-planning phase, Melissa activated the democratic decisionmaking process by reaching out to a variety of Ward 7 and 8 residents, local businesses, and organizations, requesting nominations for influential candidates. After collecting a number of suggestions, the group selected eight unique portrait subjects representing a wide variety of backgrounds, professions, hobbies, and interests. The eight selected influencers were:

1. An oral historian
2. A professional skateboarder
3. An Afro-folk singer
4. An urban farmer
5. A local assemblage artist
6. A founder of an independent activist radio station
7. A third-generation resident outreach specialist for the mayor
8. Frederick Douglass, a historical social reformer from the neighborhood, and the only nonliving portrait subject

Each portrait subject represented an enthusiastic commitment to the community, by providing their time, energy, and genuine dedication to the enhancement and service of their neighborhood.

Utilizing the connection to the university's college of art, Melissa recruited volunteer photojournalism graduate students to professionally photograph the portrait-sitters in action. She began each influencer's meeting and photo shoot with an interview in which they discussed their thoughts and experiences both as a youth and as an adult in the community. They each articulated the challenges facing their community, along with their aspirations for the neighborhood. After each meeting, the photojournalism students' photographs and interviews were taken back to the community studio at THEARC, where 30 ArtReach after-school students reflected on the portrait subjects, discussed the influencers' contributions to the community, and collaborated on brainstorming portrait materials.

Inspired by each individual, the class decided upon specific artistic media to reflect a characteristic of the portrait-sitter. Using uncommon media and processes, each portrait-sitter was depicted in a representational or symbolic form based on their relationship to the community. The local assemblage artist's portrait, for example, was made from found materials. The urban farmer's portrait comprised collaged leaves. Considering one influencer's career as the founder of a radio station, and the distinctive glasses he wore in the photograph, the students created a mosaic of cut-up vinyl records on a three-dimensional base in the shape of his glasses (see Figure 5.1). With each portrait, the students used critical thinking skills to relate to the portrait-sitters and how they could be portrayed to the community. They were urged to take risks in designing the portraits and selecting materials. With the guidance of the artist-educator, Melissa, the activities offered rigorous skill-building instruction and built competencies in a variety of portraiture media. Many of the collaborative portraits were dissected into a grid, giving each young artist a section to work on individually. The process of putting the pieces together again further signified the collaborative nature of the project, while elevating each participant's sense of contribution and responsibility.

While the young ArtReach students worked on their collaborative portraits, Melissa reached out to a group of former art students from the university by way of an alumni networking resource. As a third layer to the project, the

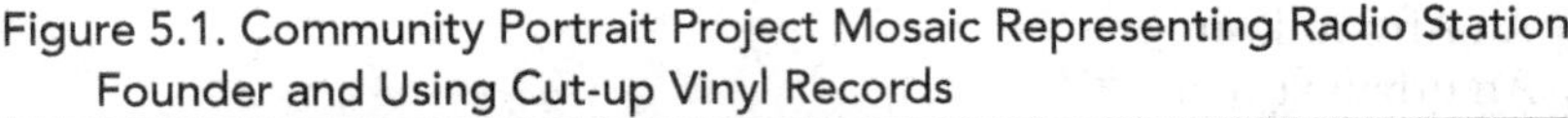

Figure 5.1. Community Portrait Project Mosaic Representing Radio Station Founder and Using Cut-up Vinyl Records

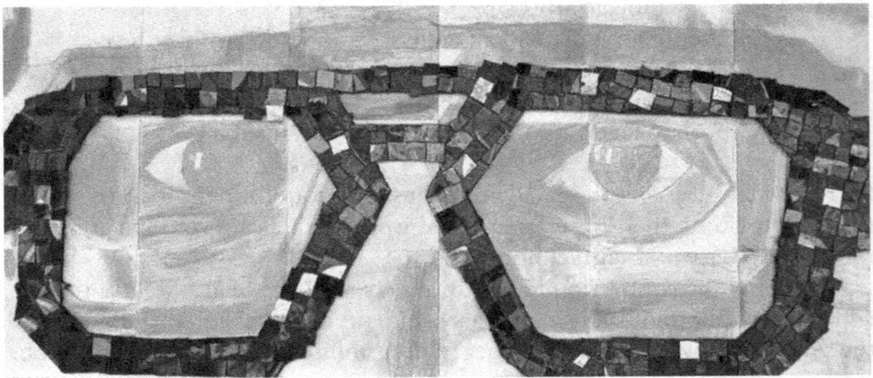

volunteer alumni artists were given photographs and interview responses of a specific influencer, and asked to create a portrait representation of that person. Working in their medium of choice, the alumni artists submitted portraits of all sizes created through painting, drawing, screen printing, linoleum cut printing, wood carving, graphic design, and sculpture. The contribution of the artist alumni portraits added to the project by exposing ArtReach students to new artistic mediums and expanding their knowledge of various techniques. The young students also identified with the older artists, no longer as spectators but as artists themselves. With the common connection and performed understanding of the shared subject matter, the parallel project provided a deeper connection between older and younger artists. The younger students came away with a greater understanding of artmaking and the many forms art careers can take.

Collaborating on a large-scale project with a number of participants working at varying speeds and fluctuating schedules proved to be a challenge. Each step of the project was dependent on the previous step to move forward. To keep a reasonable timeline, it was essential to set a clear schedule up front and send occasional reminders of exhibition deadlines. After the initial project introductions were sent out, each influencer was asked to set up a time for a photo shoot and an interview within a 2-week window. If the influencer was unavailable to participate, which happened on occasion, we were able to reach out to an alternate individual on the large list initially suggested by the community. After the photo shoots, the photojournalists returned digital copies of the portrait photographs within a week by email. Next, the photographs were emailed to the alumni artists, who committed to delivering or mailing their work in a 6-week window. During the same 6-week period the ArtReach students created a variety of portraits in the studio.

Dependence on outside volunteers can be challenging in a multitiered project. To ensure that a minimum of two portraits for each influencer was received, multiple alumni artists were assigned to each individual influencer. On occasions when an artist was no longer available to participate, Melissa was able to include additional artwork from the ArtReach students.

Nearing the end of the project, the collaborating students' portraits and alumni artist portraits were collected and put on salon-style display with the photojournalists' photographs in the ArtReach community gallery. Invitations to the opening reception were sent to 30 ArtReach students and their families, six photojournalism students, 14 alumni artists, and the seven living influencers. The project participants were particularly excited about the exhibition opening, because it would be the first time the community influencers would see the portraits and the first opportunity for all artists to meet face-to-face.

On a weekday evening, the portraits were unveiled. The gallery buzzed with excitement, and the emotion was palpable. The community influencers grinned ear-to-ear and shed tears of joy, seeing their representative portraits and meeting their doting artists. The young ArtReach students were starstruck to meet their celebrity subjects, and feverishly walked around collecting autographs. It was quite an experience to see so much mutual adoration. The opening celebration was, in itself, an inclusive and transformative experience, with incredible community participation.

The holistic project hosted opportunities to weave a fabric of the community through multiple levels of participation. Each person brought a piece of the fabric to the art project, permitting it to evolve and grow. Each participant shared a profound and enriching experience through human connection, collective pride, and interaction. The CBAE experience showcased citizens who have accomplished great things, and also helped students and the community at large understand that great things are possible.

Collaborative Garden Mural: Transforming Relationship to Place and Community

In the summer of 2016, Melissa conducted a CBAE project with a group from Wayne Place, a transitional housing residence for young adults aging out of the foster care system, to revitalize an underutilized communal outdoor space with an urban garden. Located east of the Anacostia River in Washington, DC, the low-income neighborhood was designated a *food swamp*, similar to a food desert, where families have access to high caloric processed food but limited affordable and nutritional options within walking distance. In a quest to offer residents the opportunity to participate in growing their own nutritious food, save money on produce, build social capital, and provide horticultural education, the Wayne Place staff embraced the opportunity to build an urban community garden in an underused area adjacent to the apartments.

Working with multiple organization partners, including the University of the District of Columbia's Urban Agriculture program, that specialized in educating participants in urban garden horticulture, ArtReach joined the collaboration to help build community relationships, promote civic engagement, and connect health and nutritional education through the arts. By actively engaging residents in artmaking, the goal was to establish new bonds of trust among residents, their neighbors, and the larger community, while also connecting individuals to the garden and the potential for a healthier lifestyle. With each phase of the project, participants would have opportunities to tell their story, listen to others, and add their voices, while developing an aesthetically compelling engagement space for social interaction. In designing a project that included multiple transdisciplinary goals, relationship-building was a critical step for establishing buy-in, participation, and sustained interest.

In the initial planning phase, Melissa met weekly for 2 months with the residence administration staff, participating partners, and a few residents to connect and listen to their goals, needs, and interests for the community garden. The inclusive planning ensured the community's input, fostered innovative idea generation, and furthered partnership development. As a volunteer during the garden's construction, Melissa talked with residents and neighbors and learned more about the history of the neighborhood and the passions of the residents. Using asset mapping as a tool (see Appendix A), she worked with them to identify local resources and networks, including a large group of retired veterans neighboring the building. A few of these included the open green lawn around the building, the veterans' residential facility next door, the local library, churches, schools, public parks, playgrounds, porches, faith-based meeting groups, bus stops, large trees, and historical neighborhood features.

As Wayne Place staff, ArtReach, and other partnering organizations established mutual and holistic goals for engaging the young adults and the larger community with the garden and art project, they also identified the challenges of motivating sufficient interest. With time spent in the community and multiple interactions, it was clear that the older adult neighborhood residents were excited about the idea of an accessible garden. The comments and emotions expressed by the young residents, however, revealed their skepticism regarding the unfamiliar process of gardening. The challenge became how to spark personal engagement with planting and harvesting a garden, including caring for and understanding plant growth, and connecting it with one's own nourishment. How could the arts be incorporated to speak to the community's concern about food disparity and bring about accessible opportunities to participate in the conversation? How could boxes of dirt become gathering areas for discussion, curiosity, and social cohesion?

In the project's first studio session, Melissa and volunteer participants began by finding common ground and exploring the social and cultural connections everyone has to fruits, vegetables, and herbs. The group recognized the passion shared in regard to eating, cooking, and serving food, and that each had food-related memories. There was a discussion on food and foodways that are important keys to identity. Discussing a mixture of food that was liked or disliked by various participants spurred conversations around stigmas, bad experiences, and lack of experience with select fruits and vegetables. Each participant shared their food stories and how these spoke to their culture, values, and nostalgia. The conversation topics were recorded on paper, along with the questions participants hoped the community would answer. The questions designed to excavate personal stories reflecting larger social and cultural contexts included:

- Where did you grow up and what vegetables did you eat?
- Did you have a garden? What did you grow?
- Tell us a memory you associate with a fruit or vegetable. Does a particular fruit or vegetable make you think about a person, a place, or an experience?
- Describe a vegetable you don't like. Is there a vegetable you gave a second chance to later in life?
- What fruit or vegetable would best represent your character? Why?
- How do you think a garden would impact the community?

With a revised set of food-related questions in hand, Melissa provided the resident volunteers with audio recorders and had them interview the Wayne Place staff. The dynamic shifted once the residents began to lead the conversation and spend time with the administration, learning about their personal relationships to food. With each question and response, the residents and the staff left behind their formal roles and began to connect through sharing, laughing, and listening.

The next phase of the project involved intergenerational conversations, in which residents of Wayne Place interviewed and recorded the veterans' group across the street. The process of documenting the stories of their older adult neighbors provided the residents with a new generational perspective and cultural understanding of plant-based food. The diverse stories embodied by storytellers and listeners alike offered entry points to discussions of treasured food-related memories, cultural traditions, associations, and broader food links to society. These discussions, in turn, began to awaken participants' awareness of their own relationship to food, as well as such issues as chronic disease prevention, urban renewal, food disparity, economic empowerment, and globalization.

After a few days of sharing and collecting food stories, the project group moved toward creating a collective public art piece to add to the garden. The residents brainstormed potential avenues to create an expression of communal meaning. Together they decided to create a freestanding four-sided panel sculpture, featuring resident portraits, to be centrally located in the garden. Each portrait would depict an image of the resident's food story and a wisdom word from their weekly group guidance meeting (see Figure 5.2).

The project was designed for multiple skill levels, and participation from those who did not consider themselves artists was welcomed. By identifying and building upon pre-existing strengths, the project set out to uncover the talent and inherent assets of the group. One resident had experience in tattooing and offered his lettering skills. Another resident kept a sketchbook and offered to mock up drafts for the panels. Others had little painting experience but were interested in participating with guidance. A few residents expressed not wanting to get involved in painting but offered to be part of the interview process and pose as models for the project.

Working with a local artist specializing in portraiture, the residents recruited four of their peers to be represented as icons of the garden. Holding a piece of fruit or a vegetable, the four residents individually posed in active positions while being photographed. With guidance from the local artist, the portraits were then projected onto large-scale wood panels, traced, and painted by the participants. Over the course of 2 weeks, we hosted multiple days of open studio hours where participants joined in at their leisure.

Once the portraits were complete, the residents helped carry the large, heavy panels to the garden, where they were installed (see Figure 5.3). At the evening opening and garden harvest party, all residents, staff, and neighbors

Figure 5.2. Portraits Depicting Images of Residents' Food Stories and Wisdom Words from Their Weekly Group Guidance Meeting

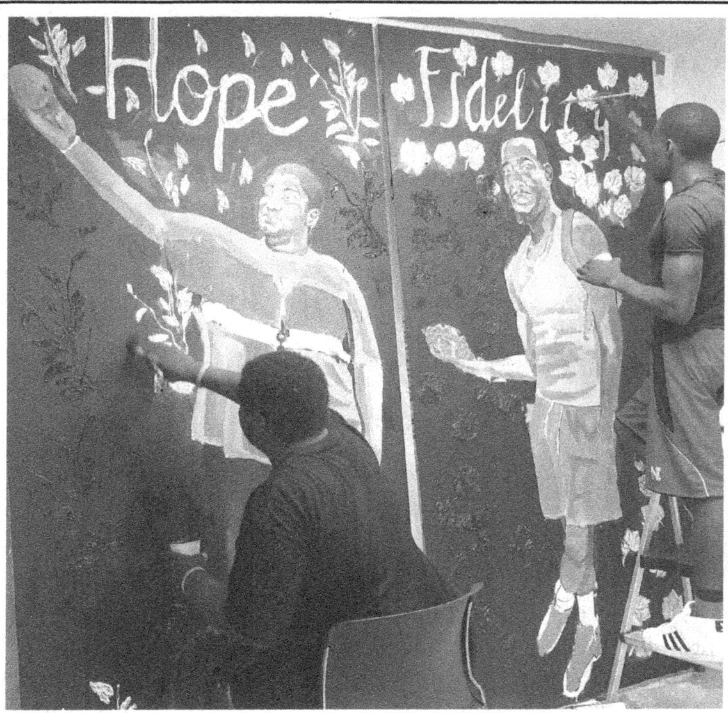

joined the celebration. The resident participants proudly shared their contributions, and the residents depicted in the portraits admired their painted representations. The artwork was a focal point of conversation, and the participants were highly regarded for their work. A few residents who had not had a chance to take part in the project due to their work schedule wanted to know when they would have a chance to participate in the future. Based on the outcome, many residents were also eager to have their portraits painted. Perhaps most humbling was the admiration of the Wayne Place staff. Many had had doubts that residents would actively engage, and were pleasantly surprised with the residents' skill and dedication, the positive peer interaction and support, and the pride and ownership expressed by those who participated.

MUTUAL GROWTH FOR COMMUNITY PARTICIPANTS, ARTIST-EDUCATORS, AND THE LARGER SOCIETY

Community engagement involves personal relationship-building, and enriches our lives by providing ways to experience the world through the eyes

Figure 5.3. Community Garden Portrait Installation

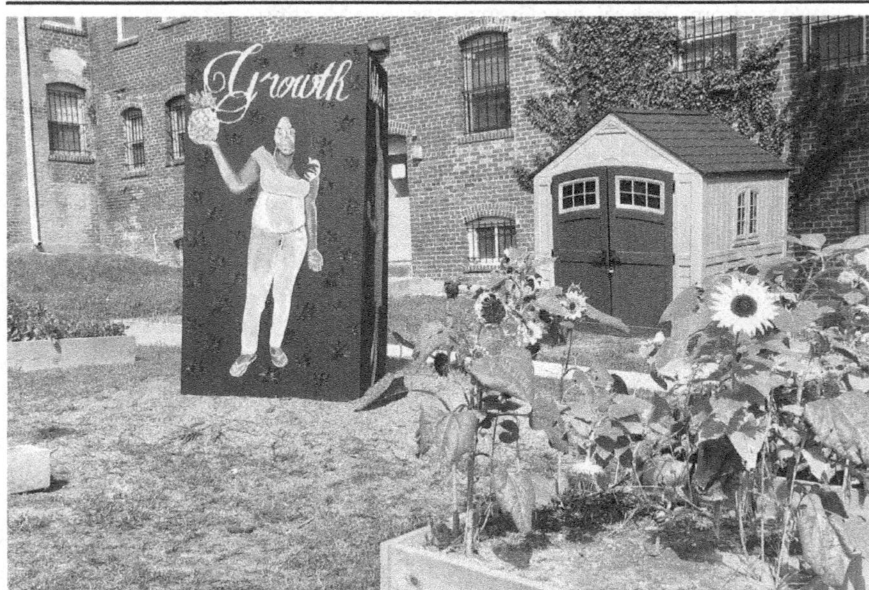

of others. One of the first and most evident opportunities of a collaborative CBAE project is the profound impact the expressive process can have on actively engaged participants, artist-educators, and the community at large. If done well, the inclusive process can foster intergenerational relationship-building, connect broader communities, develop our sense of humanity, provide an appreciation of unfamiliar cultures, challenge mainstream ideas, and promote greater social consciousness. Through conversations, open dialogue, and sharing a broad range of experiences, participants gain insight into complex perspectives, expand their perceptions, and embrace sensitive cultural translation. Throughout the process, the group builds collective efficacy through collaborative problem solving, and coming together with common interests creating a collective voice.

For the artist-educator, the partnership provides unique access to powerful engagement opportunities with the diverse cultural and historic riches of the community. CBAE projects often provide contact with a broad range of people, ideologies, educational experiences, and new ways of viewing the world that might otherwise be unknown. Seeing *process* as part of the palette, and acting as a facilitator to aid in community development, the artist-educator assists greatly in the cooperative enterprise by promoting constructive interaction and marshalling resources to a common end.

The project process can also impact and influence individual self-discovery (*educational, empowering*). Through sharing personal experiences, taking healthy risks, finding personal strengths, challenging assumptions, leaning into discomfort, embracing vulnerability, and interrogating assumptions with critical self-reflection, the expressive platform provides a space for a deeper understanding of one's own connection to existing and historical issues (*reciprocal, collaborative*).

Of course, projects designed to embrace the transformative process through connection, collaboration, and creation are first built upon respect for the diversity of the human experience (*reciprocal, transformational*). By creating curriculum with inclusive and equitable practice and multiple platforms where participants can find confidence in telling their own stories, the artist-educator aims to create an opportunity for healthy and empathetic expression and communication while developing broader global citizenship and civic engagement within select communities.

The garden mural project provided an opportunity for participants to engage in personal and communal transformation. Stakeholders had an opportunity to learn from one another through intergenerational and self-interviews and discussions; they learned about their community as situated in the larger context, promoted public awareness on a social issue, developed new art skills, strengthened engagement, and established meaningful connections among peers, neighbors, and staff. The artwork not only added aesthetic value to the underused space, but also helped create a catalyst for dialogue; illuminated core community values; increased sense of place; raised community pride; served as a gathering point to foster productive dialogue; and acted as a component for continuing opportunity and reflection.

PARTNERSHIP CHALLENGES AND OPPORTUNITIES

Forming partnerships and the iterative decisionmaking process that occurs in collaboration with your partner are the first opportunities—and sometimes challenges—in advancing the mission of the CBAE project to address the needs and assets of the community. Idea generation, project planning, and implementation are extremely time-intensive, and require a great deal of front-end preparation from everyone involved. At the beginning of Chapter 3, we discussed the process of finding a partner. In the next few pages, we want to reemphasize possible challenges and opportunities that might arise, and how to initiate and strengthen partnership formation from both the artist-educator's and the community partner's perspective.

Asset-Based Communal Identity

According to Crane (2012),

> The arts are critical components of both individual and communal identity. Some of the most important soft skills that can be used to enrich community processes

are comfort and sensitivity with cultural translations, perspectives that embrace complexity and an ability to listen and amplify critical messages. (p. 85)

Often, well-meaning collaborators focus too much on issues and problems facing a community and not enough on what makes that community unique and exemplary. Finding a community's sense of pride not only raises morale but also promotes local identity and engagement between groups. Asset mapping, described in Chapter 3, is a wonderful way to locate a variety of strengths found within a geographic location. Historical research, group discussions, interviewing, and storytelling also help gain insight into the causes and experiences of community assets and issues.

When building CBAE activities, diversity and inclusion efforts should be designed to maximize connection. Creating an environment where every individual can contribute is crucial in elevating the power of shared experiences and developing broader perspectives in participants. The project's design should foster participant learning and help them develop a deeper connection with their communities through artmaking, as well as hone skills necessary to become engaged citizens.

Through the process of identifying community aspirations, the artist-educator can help bring people together to inspire and be inspired. Shared experiences and a deepened understanding of local and relevant concerns help participants become socially conscious of the valuable contributions that actively engaged residents bring to the community, and may inspire them to enact meaningful and lasting change within their community.

The community portrait project discussed in this chapter set out to aid in the uplifting of the community's self-image. The project sought to showcase citizens who accomplished great things but also helped students believe that great things are possible. More than anything, the project was a listening process, and the exhibition was a public venue for sharing personal stories and the impetus behind the social, moral, cultural, and political concerns of the community. By highlighting the project's impact on a local level, participants have an opportunity to connect more deeply to their communities, and the exchange may encourage further social consciousness and engaged citizenship.

Collaborative Partner Selection

Of course, before being able to see these kinds of opportunities and benefits in a CBAE project, you must begin by creating a real partnership within the community. A collaborative community partner that has a genuine interest and a strong desire to partner can present a number of invaluable opportunities to the project. Many partners have a long history of collaboration, as well as flexibility in programming and the ability to respond quickly to opportunities as they arise. These partners often have strong community networks and support, which can help in areas of communication, budgeting, facilities, and so on. Most likely, the partner also has established audiences. This will allow for quick and direct communication with community members and can help build regular attendance. It is certainly a challenge to plan a weekly meeting time, only to learn that your participants have conflicting schedules or cannot attend on a consistent basis. If, for example, the partnership already has a standing meeting with a teen group after school on Tuesdays, you could tap into this preestablished time frame and guaranteed regular attendance. Another great opportunity for working with a pre-formed group is that they often have developed comfort within the facility, full procedures for dealing with emergencies, and clear ground rules in place for quicker environmental assimilation.

Partnerships with less established or formalized organizations are not always as nimble. They may have long decisionmaking timelines, fewer resources, and less available staffing for particular project needs. In many cases, these partners may have a greater need for collaboration, but they will likely require additional effort on the artist-educator's end. It is important to identify the opportunities and challenges these factors can present and how to navigate both. Regardless of the potential partner's resources, or lack thereof, if they do not have shared values or a strong desire to collaborate, your time might be better spent elsewhere. Without enthusiastic collaborators and access to community input, it will be a challenge to activate others in positive community collaboration.

In searching for a partner, the artist-educator should do his or her best to research the potential partner or communities before reaching out. During the research stage, an artist-educator should consider the partner's mission and goals:

- What are the distinctive features and capabilities of the community?
- How would a CBAE project advance the core interest and mission of the partner?
- How can you mobilize the arts to better enhance the interests of the partnership or community?
- What is the unique value that you bring to the project?
- And, again, how will the project have a meaningful impact on the community?

Once you have identified a community and/or partner organization, the next step is outreach. Remembering that community groups are often already focused on addressing immediate needs and are very busy, you will want to be clear and informative, and to share your passion for the proposed project. Leading an initial meeting or introductory email with clear objectives and project ideas helps the preoccupied partner gain a general but clear understanding of your interest, as well as an appreciation of the big picture— that is, how much the project and the time they dedicate to it might impact the community and support their mission. Understanding how the project could benefit the community will not only draw the attention of your possible collaborator but will also show the strength of your communication skills and your respect for their time. At the end of the day, the partnering group needs to prioritize what will be best for their community. When taking a risk on a new and timely collaboration, they will want to know how a partnership will support their goals, and the extent to which you will work with them to achieve them.

Wayne Place, from the second project we shared in this chapter, was a new initiative of the city's mayor, and had been up and running for under a year when Melissa reached out about the potential art project. Although they were very interested in collaborating, the staff was busy meeting the needs of their new residents and formulating institutional development. It was essential for both sides to be up front and honest with project goals and timelines. Without any available staff, they looked to Melissa to take the lead on asking questions, defining the project, recruiting participants, and carrying out the activities. To foster the community's identity, touring the facility, meeting staff, attending as many meetings as possible, and providing possible project ideas helped her create an initial structure for programming. The process evolved organically, involving participants to shape all levels of the project. With permission from the organization, the residents were encouraged to take leadership roles, take part in decisionmaking, and become active agents in the development of the project.

Building Rapport and Interpersonal Relationships

Artist-educators need to have the humility to know that they do not know what is best for the communities in which they work. The wisdom of the community comes from the community (Borwick, 2012). Outreach is often described as *for* the community, with the underlying assumption of already knowing the needs of the community; however, "to be effective, successful engagement must be done 'with' the community, based on reciprocal, mutually beneficial relationships with the organizations or communities being served" (Borwick, 2012, p. 33).

Harvesting commitment and openness within a community begins before the first meeting. Strong social connections are a necessary ingredient (Putnam, 2000). Building these connections, especially when a lack of confidence initially exists, takes time, and establishing trust takes commitment. If an artist-educator is new to the community, they may need extra time to build rapport (*reciprocal*).

A few ways to learn about the community and to express conviction is to participate and engage in community activities in advance and outside of the project whenever possible. Where does your group meet, celebrate, or socialize? Attend an event at the community center, join a church service, sit in on a public meeting, or volunteer to help at a gathering. Familiarizing yourself with the group's interests and taking time to socialize will broaden understanding of the community's identity. This also gives the group a chance to get to know you and your interest in collaboration and to gather an understanding of the CBAE project. Relationship-building is central to the project's success (*collaborative*).

In preparation for working on the garden project, Melissa spent time with the community by attending their monthly social get-togethers. At the gatherings, she had the chance to talk one-on-one with residents and staff, learning about their relationship to one another and the neighborhood. She volunteered at the community's garden-building day, putting together the raised beds and getting her hands dirty with the rest of the community planting the initial seedlings. Joining the group and spending time getting to know the members, learning their names, having a hand in the development of their community, and building sweat equity helped open dialogue and built a communal familiarity with each meeting. After a few visits, Melissa was no longer a stranger and was welcomed as part of the community. Spending the extra time to build rapport helped her learn from the community, promote greater participation, develop mutual trust and understanding, and began a productive foundation for the collaborative project.

Identifying Needs and Resources to Build Strong Participation

Enthusiastic collaborators and community participation are the project's greatest assets. Even with the help of your partnering organization, cultivating a group of participants is an obstacle for most organizers, especially when working with new constituents. By encouraging community collaboration, you are essentially blindly asking for time, patience, and perseverance, which is not a disposable energy many have or are willing to give freely. Even with the best marketing efforts, getting volunteer participants in the door might be one of the biggest challenges faced in community programming. Logistically, time and family obligations often factor in a participant's ability to attend. Organizers need to take into consideration the population they will be working with and try to identify their needs in advance. Will they need to be home to take care of family members? Are they available during weekday business hours, evenings, or weekends? Do they have meal or transportation needs? What other factors might prohibit participants from attending?

If you are working with a partnering organization, ask how it worked for them in the past. Community members have special knowledge about the individuals who live in their communities. Tap into their knowledge and brainstorm on how you might use available resources to attract volunteers. Provide the partner organization with as much advance information as possible, maintain communication, and keep an open line for suggested feedback. This will help both parties identify needs and resources to build strong participation and programming.

Sometimes, allowing participation to happen organically by hosting gatherings in a public area will open new access opportunities. Working on the garden mural project, Melissa set up the first engagement workshop on site at the housing residence. She initially planned to meet outside near the newly built garden site but, with unseasonably hot and humid weather, moved inside, setting up a few tables and tarps in the laundry room. The space turned out to be the perfect hub for recruiting participants. Not only did they have casual opportunities to engage and interview the residents during the regular workshop hours, displaying the in-progress work in the space after hours gave residents a chance to see the project evolve. The engagement and presence of an ongoing project in the communal space sparked curiosity and interest from many of the residents. Each day, more and more people joined in the project.

The sense of personal relationship or perceived direct value is also a powerful motive for participation. Generating enthusiasm and acknowledging the value of establishing a relationship will help promote curiosity and interest. Giving participants a clear understanding of the project, reasons for participation, and clear objectives at the forefront will help enhance cooperation.

In the initial meetings with the Wayne Place administrative staff, skepticism for resident interest and involvement was a concern. The staff was inclined to believe that only one or two residents, identified as predisposed to the arts, would be responsive to building and collaborating in the project. Although we often look to our partnering organizations to help recruit participants, in this case, Melissa took their advice and also shared the project far and wide in hopes of reaching residents not initially listed by the staff. Luckily, she was given a chance to talk with all residents at their monthly meeting and to share information about the project, reasons to get involved, multiple ways to join, and the value their input would have on the work. She also emphasized that it would be fun. As the project evolved and residents could see the work was being created by and for the residents with high quality and care, many joined in the process.

A Sense of Place: Creating Sustainable Opportunities for Community Involvement

According to a Gallup poll conducted in 2010, "A community's social offerings, openness, aesthetics, and education are the most likely elements to affect residents' attachment to it" (Morales, 2010, para. 1). These findings parallel the role of CBAE in the creative place-making process and collaborative expressive experiences. Building on community relationships, the garden mural project opened new avenues for dialogue between young adult residents and neighboring veterans through an exchange of narratives. Placing the collaborative murals in the public garden space also provided a unique mechanism for opening discussion and putting stakeholders in the driver's seat for broadening community revitalization efforts. Serving as a catalyst for reflection, and putting a young face on what might have been seen as an abstract issue, promoted a gathering point to bond around community identity and awareness of community concerns.

With growing community enthusiasm, the community portrait project has strong sustainable legs to continue. Expanding the list of community influencers, adding networks for nominations, furthering the democratic decisionmaking process by opening the selections to a public vote, and involving additional artists and mediums would enhance the project by not only bringing together more residents in dialogue but also broadening the celebration of dedicated, and often unseen, pillars of the community.

SUMMING UP, LOOKING AHEAD

All of the CBAE projects in this book contain their own unique opportunities and challenges as well as new ways of seeing and understanding. The wealth of each project revolved around relationship-building and collective expressions of community narratives. By being creative, we develop new ways of approaching ideas, responding to change, and being more open and flexible. Through expressive activities, we continue to explore the transformative ways in which diversity and inclusion enrich communal bonding. As you pioneer CBAE projects, consider using these tools to think anew about the community you work with and the innumerable resources they provide. By blending community into the process, you promote shared authority and authorship and foster participants in the exploration of a sense of self, a sense of place, and a sense of community (Anderson & Milbrandt, 2005). In Chapter 6 we will discuss the importance of celebrating projects through exhibitions and events.

Share/Publish/Exhibit/Celebrate
Generating Community and Developing Leaders

Making time to formally celebrate the conclusion of a CBAE project is crucial. In this phase, both process and product unify in a way that cements the community's work together, shares it with others, garners critical feedback, and plants the seeds of leadership and future collaboration. All five guiding principles of the E.R.E.C.T. conceptual framework come into play at this stage. Throughout the CBAE process, stakeholders learn about the assets and needs of their community (*educational, reciprocal*), understand how they can contribute (*collaborative, reciprocal*), develop new or refine existing art skills (*educational*), and connect with others in the act of creating (*reciprocal, empowering*). Each of these activities and opportunities generate community (*empowering*) and build leadership capacities (*transformational*).

PLANNING CELEBRATORY EVENTS

When designing a CBAE project, each phase, from selecting the community to working with the concept, tools and materials, time frame, implementation, celebration, and evaluation, needs to be considered ahead of time. How will the end product be shared? With whom? How will critical feedback be gathered and disseminated? What will be the final disposition of the artwork(s)? The planning process should be as well-considered as possible. Flexibility is key to the success of a CBAE project. Through reflexive praxis, changes to the curriculum occur throughout the process of making. Planning for where, how, and when to celebrate and share the end product needs to occur as early as possible, particularly if the plan is to exhibit artwork in a local gallery or community space. Getting your event on the calendar can take up to a year or more, depending on the venue.

Securing the Exhibit/Event Space

While it is tempting to showcase the project in a high-end space, like a gallery, it is most important to consider sites in the community itself first, to share with others who live in the community and have similar experiences, interests, concerns, and needs. Where do people in the community meet? What organizations and institutions within the community do people support? What is their capacity for hosting events? What are the costs?

Libraries tend to be places where people gather and feel comfortable regardless of race, gender, religion, ability, economic, or educational status. They are free and open to the public and "provide access to knowledge, information, lifelong learning, and works of the imagination through a range of resources and services" (Gill, 2001, p. 1). Almost every community has a public library, and many libraries have event and/or exhibition spaces. They are an excellent choice of venue to share and celebrate the results of a CBAE collaboration. They may also house special collections and archives that document the history of the community. Churches, schools, community centers, and local historical societies are also spaces that attract large numbers of people from the community. Reaching out to social/community coordinators of such organizations when planning a project to set a date for sharing the work with the broader community is an important first step.

Celebratory events should also include discussion, food and drink, and perhaps music or performance. Social media posts, handouts, and flyers outlining the purpose of the project and its participants and supporters is an effective means of spreading the word to those who may not be able to attend an opening/closing event thanking participants and supporters. Early outreach assists in determining a budget for a celebratory event. Will food be catered, or a communal potluck? Who wants to participate in a performance, discussion panel, et cetera, about the project?

In some cases, where more than one community comes together to work on a project, multiple events and sites for sharing and exhibiting the project should be considered. For example, in the case of Carving Out Freedom, several different communities participated: teens from the ArtReach program at THEARC in Washington, DC's Ward 7, adults from Wards 7 and 8, art education graduate students from the Corcoran College of Art + Design in Washington, DC, and undergraduate and graduate art and education students from the University of Maryland. A total of three exhibitions and opening events were held: at the gallery at THEARC, and at gallery spaces at the Corcoran College of Art + Design and the University of Maryland (see Figure 6.1).

Curating the Exhibition/Event

Once the space has been secured, the next step is organizing the exhibition/event. What should be included? Who should be involved in curating and installing an exhibition, and organizing performances? Curation is a skill learned through experience. The curator position is traditionally one of power, in that the curator decides what works are included and how those works are presented. In our goals for CBAE, C.A.L.L., the C, *connect, collaborate, and create*, and

Figure 6.1. Carving Out Freedom Exhibition at the University of Maryland

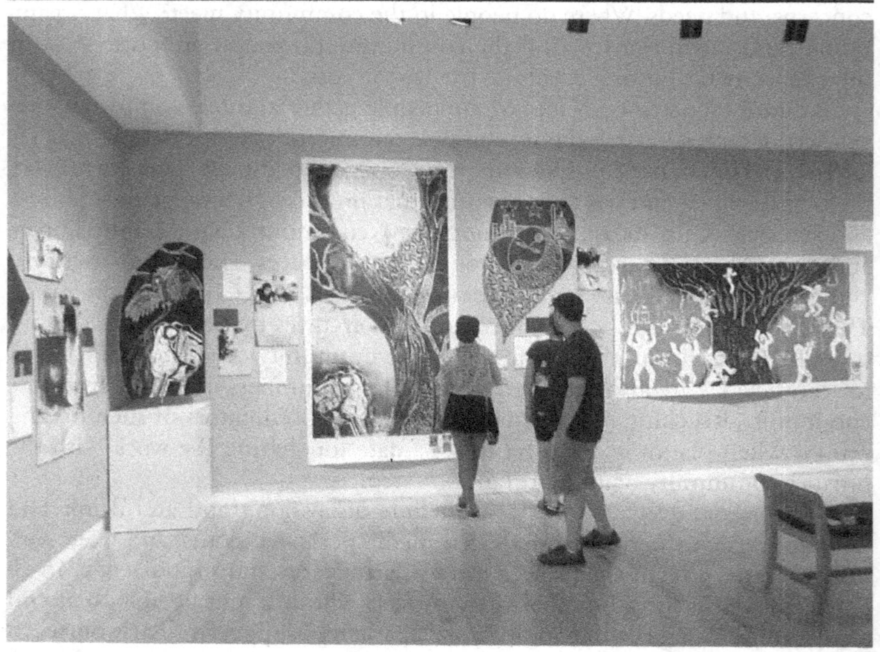

the last L, *learn and build more inclusive and equitable communities and practices*, speak to the need to invite all stakeholders to participate in the curation process. Everyone who wants to participate should have a seat at the table. The creative process and the final product are the results of a creative communal collaboration, so asking stakeholders for their opinion on what should be included and how to present it in the space provided is inclusive practice.

"There are at least four phases in any gallery-style exhibition (Burton, 2006; Hetland, Winner, Veenema, & Sheridan, 2013) requiring expertise with a variety of skill sets such as scheduling, installation/de-installation, and publicity" (Lawton, 2017, p. 100). Artist-educators "need to be conversant with each of these skills" (Lawton, 2017, p. 100), listed below, to effectively facilitate them:

1. Planning—includes curating a theme/focus; developing an exhibition team; assigning roles; securing exhibition space; coordinating schedules and timelines; selecting and preparing works for the exhibition.
2. Installation—includes designing the exhibition; preparing the physical/virtual space; creating labels and signage; installing and lighting the work.
3. Publicity—includes advertising the exhibition, posters, e-vites, postcards; hosting exhibition events, receptions, critiques, closing,

talks, and so forth; writing reviews and interviews; producing a catalog or brochure.

4. Aftermath—includes de-installing; repairing the space, organizing tools; assessing the exhibition and curating process (Burton, 2006; Hetland, Winner, Veenema, & Sheridan, 2013, cited in Lawton, 2017, p. 100).

Sharing tasks and roles is an important part of the celebration process. It also ensures that the myriad details involved in planning and installing an exhibition/event are considered, lessening the likelihood of unanticipated problems.

One of the challenges we had with the Carving Out Freedom project, despite the number of people involved, was the disposition of the large, awkwardly shaped pieces of plywood we carved to make the prints. The prints themselves were divided up among the institutional partners. Some of the woodblocks were on exhibit to provide context to viewers and insight into the entire process. A few stakeholders wanted some of the blocks, but the rest were disposed of. Perhaps if we had had more input from stakeholders at the outset, we would have found a way to preserve the wood and display it in public outdoor venues.

Documenting the Exhibition/Event and Feedback

Documentation of the celebratory event should also be considered. Just as you may have documented the project while in process and the resulting end product, you should consider documenting celebratory events. Videotaped discussions, performance, and interviews with participants and visitors are an important part of the celebratory process (Figure 6.2). They are tangible artifacts for the community and future grant funding and in-kind support. Like questionnaires and written evaluations, visual and oral documentation also provide critical feedback in assessing the value of the project goals. Documentation is your best resource for assessing a project's impact, strengths, weaknesses, and what you may want to change or repeat in the future, more of which will be discussed in the following chapter.

SUMMING UP, LOOKING AHEAD

CBAE is about teaching and learning through art in a community setting. As mentioned previously, the fluidity of teaching and learning roles within a CBAE project "empowers each individual and decentralizes decision-making. . . . It is an inherently democratic process" (Lawton, 2004b, p. 55). Creative collaboration with intergenerational stakeholders does not tend to happen in schools (Congdon, 2004; LaPorte, 2004; Lawton, 2004b); thus, creative collaboration in community and museum settings provides one of the few

Figure 6.2. Artstories RVA Alphabet Book Celebration

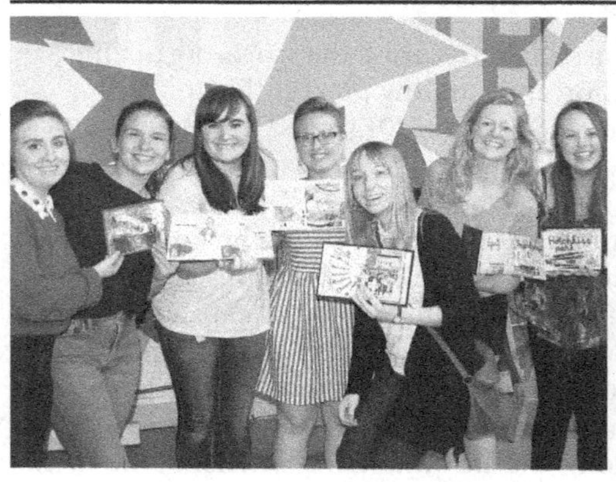

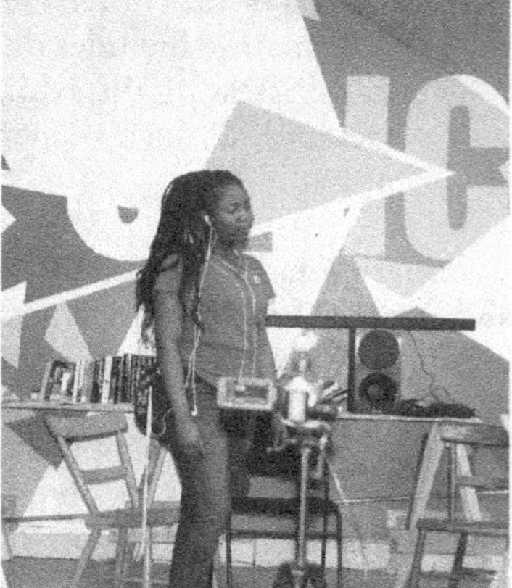

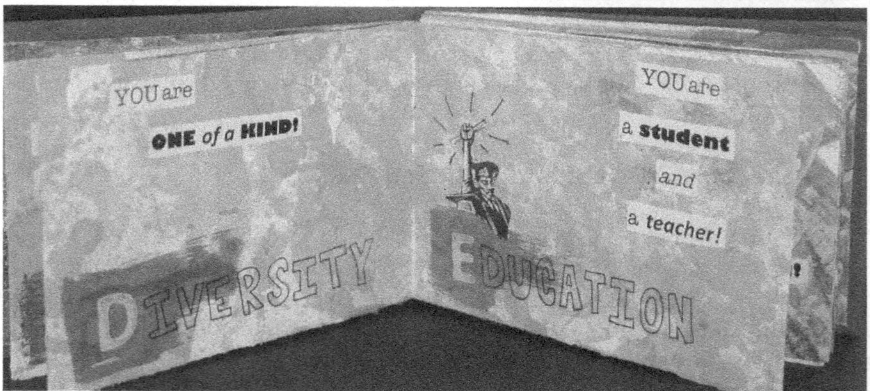

The Artstories RVA Alphabet Book Project (2018) took place during after-school hours in the Six Points Innovation Center (6PIC) located in the Highland Park community in Richmond, VA. It provided college students, their professor, youth, and adults from the neighborhood with an opportunity to collaborate on and create Richmond-themed alphabet books to promote literacy and social justice. Three different versions of the alphabet were created, one for each community partner the books were donated to. A reading of the books created was held at 6PIC that included food, music, and rap performances by the youth who collaborated on the creation of the books.

opportunities youth have for developing creative leadership capacities and connecting with older adults through art. In Chapter 1, we discuss the importance of considering the developmental characteristics of stakeholders when planning and implementing the various phases of a CBAE project. In particular, we mention Erik Erikson's (1959) theory of generativity whereby older adults take an interest in guiding the next generation. Multigenerational creative collaboration provides opportunities for generativity to occur and for young people to learn about and assume leadership roles. Once the venue for celebrating the end of a CBAE collaboration has been secured, involve stakeholders in shaping the event. If performance will be part of the celebration phase, ensure that the performers take the lead in organizing that part of the event. Older adults may be interested in planning the food and drink; college students might take the lead in promoting the event through flyers, handouts, and social media posts. The celebration phase offers as many opportunities for stakeholders to take a leadership role as participation in the creation of a CBAE project does. It also opens up possibilities for community members not involved in the CBAE project to contribute. The celebration phase broadens the impact of a CBAE project; generates community through discussion, feedback, and celebration of the work; and creates possibilities for leadership development for all stakeholders.

While the celebration phase is an enjoyable moment, it is also the ideal time to collect data needed for a final assessment of a CBAE project. If pre-assessments are conducted at the beginning, post-assessments are equally important, as they tell you what stakeholders got out of the experience. Chapter 7 discusses the importance of assessment measures in evaluating CBAE projects and suggests some best practices for developing and implementing assessments.

Assessment and Evaluation
Learning Outcomes and Enduring Understandings

Assessment and evaluation are sometimes an afterthought of the CBAE project, and it is no wonder, as it is difficult to find publications aimed at CBAE artist-educator that guide you through. Nevertheless, it is essential to gather this information to determine whether learning goals and outcomes were met, if the enduring understandings were realized, if the partnership was collaborative, and if the project is or could be sustainable. This information is not only useful for you and your stakeholders to understand the impact of the project on the participants but is often required by funders, and is useful for soliciting grants or other funding sources for future projects.

ASSESSMENT

The term *assessment* will be used to describe "a process of gathering, describing, or quantifying information" about the participants' learning or the success of the project (Oakes, Lipton, Anderson, & Stillman, 2018, p. 238). Assessment is not only important as a way to gather information about what has been learned; when they are *authentic assessments*, meaning that they are aligned with sociocultural perspectives on learning and therefore can better accommodate learners' diversity, they can also foster social justice aims (Oakes et al., 2018). Authentic assessments are not easily standardized and are difficult to use for large-scale testing purposes, but they are appropriate for CBAE projects. When assessing your CBAE project, it is important to assess both what learning has taken place, and if the project achieved the goals your team set forth at the outset. Carol Ann Tomlinson and Jay McTighe (2006), education researchers, describe various characteristics of authentic assessments: they should collect multiple forms of evidence (a photo album as opposed to a snapshot), they must measure *understanding* of the material, and they should align with the goals of learning and of how the data will be used. Revisit each of the E.R.E.C.T. principles outlined in Chapter 1, and evaluate the impact of each on the participants. Questions the assessments should answer are: Was the project:

1. *Educational?* Was it successful in providing teaching and learning opportunities for all stakeholders, artist-educators, and the broader community through art experiences, narrative co-inquiry, the public exhibition/sharing of understandings and knowledge gained, and art skills, processes and products?

2. *Reciprocal?* Did the stakeholders establish common ground whereby the contributions and voices of everyone involved were equally heard, appreciated, and considered? Did they develop rapport and value diversity? Were they inclusive, while building connections across communities of difference to effect understanding and/or meaningful change?

3. *Empowering?* Did involvement in the project and narrative co-inquiry provide opportunities for self and communal empowerment and efficacy for all participants?

4. *Collaborative?* Was the project successfully designed as a collaborative creative experience in which each stakeholder had a meaningful role to play, shared their knowledge, and cooperated in a mutually respectful manner toward the accomplishment of personal and collective goals?

5. *Transformational?* Did participating in the CBAE experience allow for the possibility of an *empowering event* (Lawton, 2004b) to occur that might lead to personal, communal, and societal transformation for the overall benefit of individuals, the community, and the broader society?

Gathering this information and discussing the results is a collaborative job as well—the information gathered will be most accurate if representatives from each of the partners work together, and it can be utilized to develop and improve upon your future CBAE projects.

Using multiple forms of assessment will give your team an accurate and nuanced picture of what participants have learned. Newman, Curtis, and Stephens (2001) evaluated the impact of creative arts programming in the United Kingdom that was aimed at socially excluded youth. They did this through a thorough literature review of published documents that included evaluations of community arts programming with "adequate description(s) of their methodology" (p. 6). These methodologies are commonly used to evaluate CBAE projects, and include the following:

- Pre- and post-project interviews with participants, formal and informal
- Direct observations
- Pre- and post-project questionnaires completed by participants
- Self-reporting by the organizers

- Surveys of community participants
- Instructor assessments; written documentation from community arts projects
- Discussion or focus groups with funders, artists, and participants
- Written documentation from projects

We would add *visual journals* and *artwork* to this list of tools that will be useful for your data-gathering. Following are descriptions of the various aspects of assessment, some examples of these assessment tools that are useful for CBAE projects, and explanations of when and why particular ones might be useful for different projects.

Criteria

To create authentic assessments, you will need to be sure you know what you are assessing. Refer back to the goals you identified at the outset of the project, and create criteria for your assessments to reflect these goals. This will help keep the assessments clear, relevant, and integrated, and, with any luck, they will be an engaging addition to the project instead of a seemingly arbitrary or laborious task. When using assessments of participant learning, the criteria should be shared with the participants, because "by attending to the criteria, students tend to focus on what is important, and accordingly their learning is enhanced ... It is the awareness of the criteria ... that promotes such learning" (Stewart & Walker, 2005, p. 95). When the criteria are linked to the learning goals, the information you gather will give you a true understanding of the learning that is or is not occurring.

Developing the Assessment

In their 2005 book *Rethinking Curriculum in Art*, authors Marilyn Stewart and Sydney Walker have created a useful and thorough checklist for art teachers to assess for students' understanding in a classroom setting. Here is a brief version of their checklist that we've adapted for CBAE projects:

1. *Identify the purpose of the assessment*—does it assess the following topics: stakeholders' prior knowledge? How things are going in the project? What have stakeholders learned so far? Their attitudes about participating in the project? How the various stakeholders feel about the collaboration?
2. *Clarify what it is that you wish to assess*—are you interested in learning about the stakeholders' skill development? Developing an understanding of the project theme or enduring understandings? How the stakeholders feel about their role in the project? Did each stakeholder feel as though they played an important role in the project?

3. *Brainstorm ideas for possible ways in which stakeholders can demonstrate learning throughout the project*–from your past experience working with others, what strategies have worked for you to gather information about what was learned at various stages? Are there strategies you have not utilized before that might work well with this project? Are there mini-projects stakeholders might engage in that will scaffold their learning—a journal entry, scratchboard drawing, foam print, written or visual response to a prompt?

4. *From your brainstorming session, select a list of strategies or projects that will best serve to elicit an understanding or a skill you wish to assess—*make sure that each one relates to one of your goals; is focused on a skill or understanding you have identified; is authentic, relating to the stakeholders and their interests; is realistic in your time frame, considering your materials and resources; and can be completed by all stakeholders.

5. *Determine criteria for assessment*—what will count as successful completion of the performance task? What criteria will demonstrate learned skill or understanding?

For those interested in the complete checklist as originally conceived, please see Stewart and Walker's book (2005, p. 101).

Assessment of Learning: Formative and Summative

While the traditional expectation of assessment is that it is done after a project is complete, in reality, assessment begins at the beginning. Assessment of learning in a CBAE project is a continual process that starts with *identifying* clear instructional goals at the outset of the project, *articulating* these goals to the stakeholders, *responding* to stakeholders' needs and giving feedback, and encouraging *reflection* throughout the duration of the project. Therefore, the best assessments are not additional work to be done once your project is displayed, but information that is gathered throughout the entire process.

Formative Assessments. These assessments are ongoing and include observations, summaries, and reviews that inform instruction and provide stakeholders with feedback daily (Fisher & Frey, 2014). Formative assessments refer to "judgments made during the implementation of a program that are directed toward modifying, learning or improving the program, before it is completed" (Beattie, 1997, p. 4). They have traditionally been used throughout an educational experience to measure what was learned up to a particular point in time, and are used more to assess *for* learning, meaning that they support instructors in knowing what has or has not been learned, so they can adjust their teaching to address the needs of the learners—formative assessment is a support for learners during the learning process (Stiggins, 2007). In this way, formative assessment is a diagnostic tool to monitor what is being learned and which strategies are working, and provides ongoing feedback to the instructors to adjust their teaching based on the results of the assessment. In the case of CBAE projects, they should be quickly and seamlessly incorporated into the project. These assessments work in concert with *diagnostic* assessments, which are designed to gather students' prior knowledge and understandings before beginning the project (Oakes et al., 2018). Examples of diagnostic assessments include tools such as pre-project questionnaires and interviews.

One useful example of a formative assessment that can be used with CBAE is the *Teaching for Understanding* framework, or TfU. TfU was developed at the Harvard Graduate School of Education and is a framework that CBAE artist-educators can use to shape the learning that is taking place in the project. It is used in the planning stages of the project, throughout the studio process, and finally for use in evaluating the learning that occurred.

Adapting the TfU framework for teaching for CBAE, practitioners would follow these steps:

1. Generate a topic that connects with the participants;
2. Create understanding goals—specifying what participants should learn about a topic;
3. Create understanding performances—activities that will display and advance learners' understanding; and
4. Engage in ongoing assessment—assessment practices that provide timely and frequent feedback for learners' activities throughout the learning process.

In essence, you should ask four main questions before you begin the project: What topic is relevant to the stakeholders? What is worth understanding about this topic? How will we engage the stakeholders in this understanding? How will they show their understanding, and how might we guide them to develop a deeper understanding?

A vital component of the TfU framework is that of ongoing assessment. When designing the assessment, be sure to abide by this outline:

- Create clear and explicit criteria for performance;
- Ensure that assessment occurs frequently;
- Gather multiple sources of feedback;
- Use it to gauge progress and inform planning. (Perkins, 1993)

Summative Assessment. As a complement to the formative assessments that help shape the project while in progress, summative assessments are "used at the end of a course or segment of learning, for the purpose of summarizing what students know and are able to do, and are in conjunction with ... criteria" (Beattie, 1997, p. 84). Some examples of useful summative assessments are:

- Interviews
- Observations
- Pre- and post-project interviews with participants, formal and informal
- Pre- and post-project questionnaires completed by participants
- Self-reporting by the organizers
- Surveys of stakeholders
- Instructor assessments; written documentation from community arts projects
- Discussion or focus groups with funders, artists, and stakeholders
- Written documentation from projects

In her CBAE courses, Pamela routinely uses visual reflection journals (see Figures 4.3 and 4.6) as a form of summative assessment for her students. Using the Kolb model of experiential learning, students reflect in writing and with visual examples on their collaborative community experience in four phases as follows:

1. *Concrete Experience* is characterized by doing. In the concrete experience stage, learners must be able to involve themselves in new experiences fully, openly, and without bias.

   In journaling a concrete experience, use purely descriptive terms to describe a significant event that happened in working with your community partners (who, what, where, when, how many, etc.).

2. *Reflective Observation*—review, re-see, mentally revisit the concrete experience.

   This is affective action—in your journal, write about the feelings and emotions you experienced while the concrete event was occurring.

3. *Abstract Conceptualization*—interpretation of the concrete experience and reflective observation in light of other learning, theories, or related concepts (readings, class discussions).

   For your journal entry, state what conclusions you have drawn from your concrete experience and reflective observation. Write about what you learned about yourself and others as a result of this experience.

4. *Active Experimentation*—Translate new understandings into action or plan what action will occur next. Here newly developed understandings and theories guide new experiences.

   In your journal, list your action plans based on the above three sections.

   If this event or a similar one were to occur in the future, how would you respond?

(adapted from Kolb's experiential learning model, 1984)

Community members are asked to complete a post-activity questionnaire, and in the case of CBAE research, interviews are conducted with some of the stakeholders to evaluate what they learned from the experience and how it could be improved.

EVALUATING THE COLLABORATION

In addition to gauging what stakeholders learned throughout the CBAE project, it is also important to evaluate how successful the collaboration was. Evaluation is how we interpret the performance of the participants or the success of the project (Oakes et al., 2018). It involves "applying established criteria to determine the quality, value, or worth of the performance" (Oakes et al., 2018, p. 240) or project success. The results of the assessments help you evaluate the project. This will teach you much about how to design and approach future collaborations, as well as give you data for post-project conversations with the partners as well as funders, and will be useful when writing reports or grant proposals for future projects.

Like the formative and summative assessments for understanding the learning and attitudes of the participants, you should evaluate the collaboration by starting at the beginning—with the goals you and your partners set forth for a successful collaboration. In *Collaboration Among Professionals, Students, Families and Communities: Effective Teaming for Student Learning* (Richards, Frank, Sableski, & Arnold, 2016), the authors recommend using what they coined the SMART objective approach to identifying specific tasks for different members of the team (Richards et al., 2016, p. 22). SMART stands for *specific, measurable, ambitious, realistic,* and *time-oriented*. At the outset of the project, design goals for the partnership, including working within the timeline and budget, sharing decisionmaking equally, creating and implementing assessments, deciding what enduring understandings you expect the stakeholders to acquire, and so on that meet the SMART objectives. These may be shared goals, such as creating pre- and post-questionnaires together, or goals that are divided between the partners. To stay on target with the project time frame, it is helpful to create a timeline of the goals, with the name of the partner or partners who will take responsibility for each. This will also be invaluable at the end when evaluating the success of the partnership.

To assess the goals of the partnership, Richards and colleagues (2016) recommend a two-level approach. First, assess whether the partnership was collaborative and the process successful and equitable. This can be done through conversations about the success of the collaboration, "what barriers were met, what strengths assisted the team, whether the process allowed for all members to participate meaningfully, and so on" (Richards et al., 2016, p. 23). It is important to listen to all perspectives on these matters, and determine if every stakeholder feels their role was supported and that they each accept responsibility for the outcomes. Whether or not this is the case, this is valuable information for your evaluation.

If it is determined that the partnership was collaborative and equitable, the second level is to evaluate its success in fulfilling the goals established at the start. As you are likely designing a small-scale collaboration with a handful of people at the helm of the partnership, this can be done in a post-project meeting as opposed to more formal assessments such as surveys. As before, be certain to take an objective approach to the goals set forth, and ensure that all partners in the collaboration have equal say in the discussion. What did each partner value most? What did they learn? What was the most challenging aspect of the collaboration? How might data from the learning assessments (such as pre-/post-activity surveys, interviews, in-process observations, and other feedback) be utilized to develop and improve upon future CBAE projects? What would they change if developing future CBAE projects? Finally, is the project sustainable? That is, can it continue running on its own once the organizations step out? And should it be? If so, what can be done to ensure its sustainability? These are all important questions for you and the other partners to consider. Arts Victoria (2013), a government body in the state of Victoria, Australia, dedicated to supporting, championing, and growing the state's creative industries, developed a work guide for artists working in the community, with a useful list of questions to guide evaluation. An evaluation that answers these and the earlier questions would be very thorough, and useful in designing future projects, reporting to grant organizations, and helpful in ensuring funding in the future (https://www. vichealth.vic.gov.au/).

Once finished, the results of this evaluation of the CBAE partnership should be recorded in writing and shared with all stakeholders. Figure 7.1 provides a sample evaluation plan for CBAE. This plan aligns with the Five Critical Levels of Professional Development Evaluation (Guskey, 2000) and is adapted here to show how project goals/criteria can be aligned with formative and summative assessments.

SUMMING UP, LOOKING AHEAD

For assessment and evaluation to be most effective, they should be included in the initial planning stages of the project. In this way, they will guide the design of the project as well as the method of instruction. This will ensure that you meet your learning goals and outcomes and achieve enduring understandings, will guarantee that the partnership was collaborative, and will assist in determining the sustainability of the project. This invaluable information will guide and shape the process during learning, will help you understand the impact of the project on the participants, and will be valuable data for soliciting grants or other funding sources for future projects.

Collecting assessment and evaluation data is the bookends to your project—it starts at the very beginning, and once it is completed, so is the project. This may be a moment of regret that it is over, but you can look back and you can see the great learning that has occurred and feel proud of the hard work you all put into this great venture!

Figure 7.1. Sample CBAE Assessment Rubric

GOALS/CRITERIA FOR ASSESSMENT If you're interested in knowing:	Suggested tools for FORMATIVE ASSESSMENT (including diagnostic)	Suggested tools for SUMMATIVE ASSESSMENT
Did participants acquire new skills and knowledge in the art form?	☐ Direct observation ☐ Visual journal and artworks ☐ Self-reporting	☐ Post questionnaires ☐ Visual journal and artworks ☐ Self-reporting
Did participants engage creatively in solving artistic and instructional problems?	☐ Direct observation ☐ Visual journal and artworks ☐ Self-reporting	☐ Post questionnaires ☐ Visual journal and artworks ☐ Self-reporting
Did the participants develop an understanding of the project theme or enduring understandings?	☐ Pre interviews, formal and informal ☐ Visual journal and artworks ☐ Pre questionnaires ☐ Direct observation ☐ Self-reporting ☐ Concept mapping	☐ Post interviews, formal and informal ☐ Visual journal and artworks ☐ Post questionnaires ☐ Self-reporting ☐ Concept mapping
How do the participants feel about their role in the project?	☐ Pre interviews, formal and informal ☐ Pre questionnaires ☐ Direct observation ☐ Self-reporting	☐ Post interviews, formal and informal ☐ Post questionnaires ☐ Self-reporting

Figure 7.1. Sample CBAE Assessment Rubric (continued)

GOALS/CRITERIA FOR ASSESSMENT If you're interested in knowing:	Suggested tools for FORMATIVE ASSESSMENT (including diagnostic)	Suggested tools for SUMMATIVE ASSESSMENT
Was the content relevant?	☐ Pre interviews, formal and informal ☐ Pre questionnaires ☐ Direct observation ☐ Self-reporting	☐ Post interviews, formal and informal ☐ Post questionnaires ☐ Self-reporting
Were the objectives implemented and achieved?	☐ Direct observation ☐ Visual journal and artworks	☐ Post interviews, formal and informal ☐ Visual journal and artworks ☐ Post questionnaires
Did participants work collaboratively?	☐ Direct observation ☐ Self-reporting	☐ Post interviews, formal and informal ☐ Post questionnaires ☐ Self-reporting
Did the physical space support learning?	☐ Direct observation ☐ Self-reporting	☐ Post interviews, formal and informal ☐ Post questionnaires
Was the experience well-organized?	☐ Direct observation ☐ Self-reporting	☐ Post interviews, formal and informal ☐ Post questionnaires
How did the partners feel about their role in the project? What did each partner value most? What did they learn? What was the most challenging aspect of the collaboration? What would they change if developing future CBAE projects?	☐ Self-reporting	☐ Post interviews, formal and informal ☐ Post questionnaires ☐ Self-reporting

Conclusion

CBAE is education for action with art as the medium for learning.

Since we embarked on this journey to compile our experiences and ideas regarding CBAE into a book that we hope is both informative and useful, the need for community-based work to heal breaches, build bridges, foster inclusivity, and develop understanding and empathy has greatly increased. The divisive nature of current politics in the United States (and elsewhere) has created alarming tensions between people reaching for the American Dream and those who believe their dreams and values are threatened.

CBAE is about finding inroads through arts learning that help stakeholders from a variety of backgrounds, experiences, and ideologies to find common ground. As human beings, we not only share the same spaces, but also the same needs and wants: equal opportunity and fairness in securing a safe place to live and care for loved ones; access to high-quality education; equal pay for equal work; access to quality goods and services such as health care, food, and so forth to sustain us; and the right to pursue happiness and live our lives as we see fit within the rule of laws that are fair, just, and equitable.

Focusing on the assets each stakeholder brings to a partnership and ensuring that each participant has a voice in the entire process from start to finish is one way to establish common ground, build community, and foster transformative experiences leading to increased understanding and empathy.

This book attempts to provide the reader with the tools and resources needed to develop partnerships; design experiences that build on community assets, interests, and needs; and teach art skills and ways of communicating (visual, oral, written, and performed) that can be personally and communally transformative and sustainable.

We wrote this book primarily for artist-educators and researchers with an interest in activism, creative place-making, community-building, creative youth development, transformative learning, and intergenerational learning through art. The examples provided come from our own experience designing and implementing CBAE programs, and the challenges and opportunities we faced in facilitating age-integrated art curriculum with diverse learners in a variety of settings. Our examples are those of artist-educators connected to higher education and museums. Therefore, our perspective is limited, as it does not include the voices of our nonprofit community partners as authors.

We hope K–16 artist-educators will find the ideas here useful in involving their students in CBAE, taking the school out to community spaces, and bringing the community into school spaces. With this in mind, we include examples of CBAE curriculum for K–16 educators required to include standards in their curriculums (see Appendixes E and F for standards-based curriculum plans).

For the teaching artist and community-based artist-educator working with youth, aging, and intergenerational populations, we include examples of curriculum using our age-integrated curriculum theory and E.R.E.C.T framework as a guide for designing CBAE experiences that consider the educational, developmental, and psychosocial needs of stakeholders (see Appendixes B and C).

For artist-educator researchers, we include qualitative arts-based research methodologies that pair well with CBAE programming. We purposefully organized the text so that artist-educators with little or extensive experience with CBAE will find the ideas expressed here useful.

For nonprofit artist-educators and administrators, we hope our text will assist in reaching out to K–16 education partners to develop sustainable relationships through CBAE programming.

The book is designed to be read in sequential order; however, if the reader just wants to know what theories connect with CBAE, they can easily get what they need in Chapters 1 and 2. If the reader is interested in ensuring that they haven't missed crucial steps in the CBAE planning process, they may just want to reference Chapters 3 and 4. Perhaps anticipating what opportunities and challenges may arise is of interest—in that case, Chapter 5 is helpful. In other words, each chapter can stand alone depending upon the needs of the reader.

Our CBAE principles, educational, reciprocal, empowering, collaborative and transformative (E.R.E.C.T), are the building blocks for comprehensive CBAE programs, with the goal of **C**onnecting, collaborating and creating through **A**rt-based, asset-centered activity, to **L**isten to the stories of others in order to **L**earn and build more inclusive and equitable communities and practices (C.A.L.L).

Finally, we include online resources (Appendix D), curriculum (Appendixes E and F), and sample CBAE proposals (Appendixes G and H) to aid the reader in creating CBAE programs that are sustainable; open critical dialogue through narrative art forms; and develop learning goals, enduring understandings, and assessments that foster personal and socially transformative arts learning experiences.

Community Asset Map Template

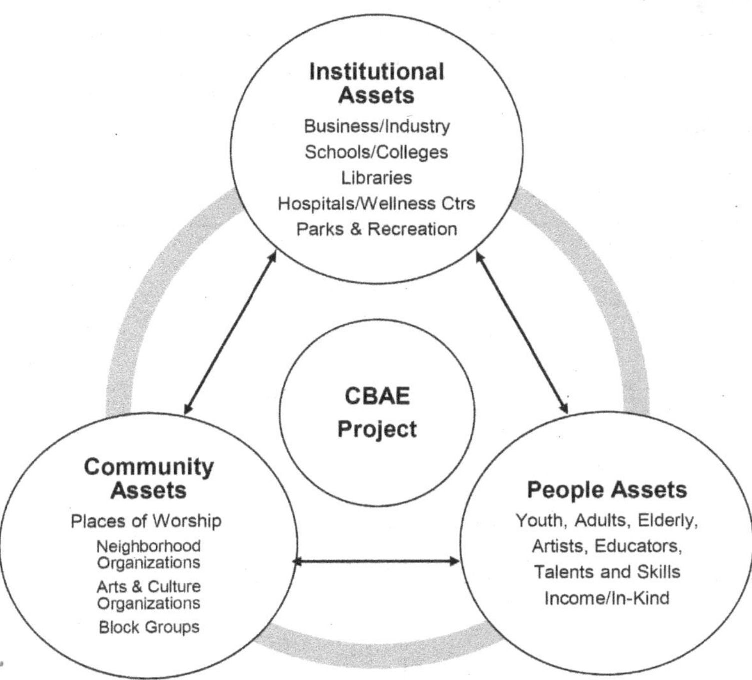

Asset-based community development (ABCD) uses five key community assets: individuals, associations, institutions, physical assets, and connections. Chart adapted from the ABCD approach developed by John L. McKnight and John P. Kretzmann (1993) at Northwestern University, Evanston, IL.

Age-Integrated Curriculum Plan Template (pg. 1)

Age-Integrated Curriculum Plan	
Title:	**Stakeholder Age Range:**
Community Assets: Based on asset mapping, list resources available within the community (people, places, materials)	
Stakeholder Creative Development Stage(s): Cohen and Kerlevage	**Stakeholder Psychosocial Stage(s):** Erikson's stage(s)
E.R.E.C.T. Project Principles: **Educational:** Art skills taught; knowledge/skills sought	**Reciprocal:** Rapport/trust-building activities; team activities
Empowering: Co-inquiry process; activities for sharing and listening	**Collaborative:** List roles available for stakeholders
Transformative: Empowering events planned	**Project Description:** Describe the project: What will stakeholders do?
Materials: List all materials needed to implement the project	

Age-Integrated Curriculum Plan Template (pg. 2)

Essential Questions: What questions do stakeholders have/want to address through the art process? These should be connected to the generative theme.	**Enduring Understandings:** What should stakeholders understand, remember, and be able to apply in other aspects of their lives?

ACTIVITY SCHEDULE		
DATE	TIME	ACTIVITY

Flexibility Plan: Describe how you plan to build flexibility into your curriculum---for example if not all stakeholders show up what will you do? If they want to do something different? What are your contingency plans?

Outcomes/Assessment: Plan for assessing the impact of the project. A celebratory event, interviews, surveys, reflection journal.

Artist-Educator Reflection: What went well? What didn't? What should change next time? How will you sustain the partnership?

Sample Age-Integrated Curriculum Plan for *Carving Out Freedom* (pg. 1)

Age-Integrated Curriculum Plan	
Title: *Carving Out Freedom*	**Stakeholder Age Range:** 10-70

Community Assets: Project to be held at THEARC, a community space with a variety of non-profit partners catering to all ages, including a neighborhood representative office. There is a community gallery to show art work, studio art room, community garden, and farmers market. The parking lot has plenty of space to set-up steamroller printing. The Farmers Market takes place on Saturdays and printing on a Saturday pulls in more community members to participate. THEARC is a very busy space and the Partner organizations are willing to help recruit participants from the neighborhood. In addition, the ArtReach program at THEARC has a studio classroom they are willing to let us use between 4:30-7:30pm, Tuesdays and Thursdays and will allow us to leave unfinished artworks and supplies safely secured in the room.

Stakeholder Creative Development Stage(s): Given the age range 10-70, two stages of artistic development are represented: *emerging expertise* and *artistic thinking*. The 10-year old is in the emerging expertise stage—moving beyond representative schema and is interested in improving art skills –making more realistic art. There is also and interest in social issues at this stage. The college aged students are in the *artistic thinking* stage where art is a creative process; social issues provide motivation to make art. A personal style has developed; ability to think abstractly. *Mid-life re-evaluation stage*, 3+ participants have a capacity for introspection and seek gratification through creative endeavor. *Liberation Phase*—confidence in knowledge gained over a lifetime, interest in creative experimentation.	**Stakeholder Psycho-Social Stage(s):** One 10-year old, his 16 year year old brother and 19-year friend fall into the *identity vs identity confusion*. For the 10-year old there is an interest in connecting with new experiences. Making a large woodcut and writing poetry will provide new experiences in making art and in making art with a group of people; collaboration. The teens are transitioning to adulthood and working with adults of various ages on common ground. The opportunity to talk/work with adults provides much support. *Generativity vs. stagnation*—the artist-educators and 2 + participants feel the need to help guide the next generation in art and to feel successful and affirmed. *Efficacy vs passivity*-feel the need to influence through lived experience. *Investment vs Detachment*-heightened perceptions of meaning and significance for one's belongings, surroundings, personal relationships; increased appreciation for one's life.
E.R.E.C.T. Project Principles: **Educational:** Focusing on our theme, *freedom*, participants are asked to share their personal definition of freedom. College students met for 2 weeks to discuss theory , definition, and history of community-based art education, look at woodcuts and artworks about freedom (N. Rockwell) and experiment with relief printmaking processes on a small scale. College students also discussed their ideas for CBAE proposal writing assignment for the class.	**Reciprocal:** Begin with opportunities for people to share a bit of their personal story, past art experiences, and current art interests. College students meet for 3 weeks prior to community stakeholders to complete life story and identity maps and consider how their biases may impact their learning and collaboration with one another and community stakeholders. As 2 college groups were involved they learned to respectfully listen and respond to one another in preparation for meeting/working with community stakeholders.
Empowering: The first meeting with the community and college students provides opportunity to establish common ground, learn to respectfully listen and respond to one another. The different roles involved with the project are explained and stakeholders decide what roles are meaningful and of interest to them and if none are, flexibility in developing role(s) that make them feel empowered is crucial.	**Collaborative:** All stakeholders engage in a collaborative brainstorming activity, creating a word web with *freedom* as the focus. Next stakeholders selected words they thought could be grouped together. Then stakeholders decide which grouping of words they want to work with to envision a visual representation of freedom. Stakeholders group themselves based on the word grouping they want to work with and collaborate with one another on creation of a unified sketch to transfer to wood and begin carving.
Transformative: The relationships stakeholders develop in working with one another on a theme of personal, social, and communal significance can lead to a transformation in attitudes regarding difference (age, race, etc). Working with unfamiliar art materials and people one doesn't normally encounter, can lead to an empowering event, transforming stakeholders attitudes and perspectives about art and people.	**Project Description:** Three 4' x 8' foot woodcuts will be created, 3 by stakeholder groups and 1 by the artist-educators. The woodblocks will be cut into 5 pieces so each stakeholder has their own piece to carve that will then be connected to the other pieces their group in a large jig and printed as one unified work. Several sets of prints for exhibition in 3 venues will be printed. A poetry workshop with templates to assist each stakeholder in writing their own freedom poem for exhibition. A video of some stakeholders discussing their thoughts on freedom will be produced and exhibited with prints.

Materials: Paper for sketches, large printmaking paper for printing, four, 4'x8' pieces of plywood for carving images. Woodcut gouges, Dremel tools and safety goggles, sand paper, carbon paper for transferring images, liquid water color to paint onto uncut woodblocks, mix of varsol and shellac to varnish wood, oil based ink in several colors, large felt blankets for printing, rented steamroller, brayers, large pieces of plexiglass for rolling out ink, baby oil and mineral spirits, rags, and nitrile gloves for clean-up. Scratch board and small linoleum blocks for practice with relief printing processes. Video camera, tripod, and camera to photo document throughout the process.

Sample Age-Integrated Curriculum Plan for *Carving Out Freedom* (pg. 2)

<table>
<tr><td>

Essential Questions:
What can we learn about effective art teaching practices through participation in a CBAE project? What similarities and differences do we discover and what can we learn about effective CBAE? What can we learn about ourselves as educators, artists, researchers, and concerned citizens working in partnership with an intergenerational community of learners? How do the lessons we learn in the act of researching/artmaking/teaching/metacognitive reflection impact, change, or influence the construction/reconstruction of our own identities? How will this communal experience influence our thinking about learners from other cultures, backgrounds, traditions and our artmaking and teaching practice?

</td><td>

Enduring Understandings:
Knowledge of educational theory and practice that engage and empower learners and communities. Developing understanding of issues of diversity, inclusion, privilege and power. Exploration of personal values, ethics, and ideologies. Developing understanding of service-learning, transformative learning, and CBAE. Art, including broad education in visual art/visual culture, is an important integrated component of contemporary society, a global form of communication that crosses socio-economic, ethnic, ideological, racial, cultural and aesthetic boundaries. Personal engagement in the making and studying of visual art and culture both individually and cooperatively contributes to the search for meaning and value in the world.

</td></tr>
</table>

ACTIVITY SCHEDULE		
DATE	**TIME**	**ACTIVITY**
Week 1	4:30-7:30	College students from both colleges meet, journey map/identity map assignments. Assign group readings for students to present (CBAE, transformative learning, service-learning, intergenerational learning and art making). Practice with scratch board in preparation for wood cuts.
Week 2	4:30-7:30	Presentation on readings; begin prepping altered books for reflections; Show images of prints and artworks on the theme of *freedom*.
Week 3	4:30-7:30	First meeting with stakeholders from the community. Introduction activity. Sharing narratives of experience. Brainstorm word web on Freedom, begin envisioning process. Break into small groups based on word grouping interests. Photographer take some photos of work in progress.
Week 4	4:30-7:30	Small groups begin the envisioning process, creating visual imagery for the words they selected, drafting a final design. Groups share their final sketches with artist-educators who then asks them how they want their wood cut into pieces (5 pieces one for each person in the group to carve).
Week 5	4:30-7:30	Stakeholders transfer their drawings onto the wood and artist-educators review safe tool use. Wood blocks are sanded and dyed with water color. Carving begins.
Week 6	4:30-7:30	Carving finalized and proof prints made. Preparations for printing in the parking lot on a Saturday morning are made. Saturday morning/farmers market day stakeholders set up tables outside for inking blocks and ink and place blocks into printing jig. Assistance from volunteer bystanders with laying paper and blankets over the paper. Instructions on how to drive the steamroller over the prints. Everyone inks and prints! Videos finalized, edited

Flexibility Plan: After explaining the roles, goals and purpose of the project, ask participants what they want to work with. Some may not feel confident or interested in carving the wood, but may want to help with the brainstorming and envisioning process. Some may want to be more involved in the writing, poetry activity. Others may want to work on producing the video. Some may be interested in the printing part of the project, inking wood plates, prepping paper for printing, driving the steamroller to print and laying out prints to dry. Or they may see their role in curating, designing the exhibition/reception/celebration phase.

Outcomes/Assessment: For college students, altered book reflections that demonstrate their learning throughout the process, and written proposals and poetry. Formative assessment —observation of collaborative/reciprocal learning within groups. Collaborative rubric. Assistance with the exhibitions in 3 venues: THEARC Gallery, and gallery spaces at each college for 3 simultaneous exhibitions. Post activity questions to capture stakeholders' thoughts on the entire process, pros, cons, what they learned, what they would do differently, etc.

Artist-Educator Reflection: It was amazing to see how a 10-year old and a 70-year old worked with art education students and education students to create a very well-crafted vision of freedom, each stakeholder cut their own piece and assisted others in finishing. The artist-educators also had a chance to collaborate as well as assist stakeholders. The entire process was complex, but went off without a hitch. One stakeholder was not interested in artmaking, but became very involved in directing the video. The only "problem" was what to do with large odd shaped pieces of wood (some were part of the exhibition) after the project ended. Unfortunately, some pieces were trashed, others stakeholders wanted to take away with them.

Online Resources

www.teachersforjustice.org/

Teachers for Social Justice (TSJ) is a Chicago-based K–20 organization committed to education for social justice. They have regular meetings to discuss, develop, and collaborate on curriculum that is anti-racist, multicultural, multilingual, and grounded in student experience. They are also involved in sociopolitical activism to support the voices of educators in school policy.

https://www.americansforthearts.org/

ArtsBlog is a blog for Americans for the Arts written by leading experts in the field. It features topics covering everything from arts education to public art to community engagement through arts and more.

www.kappanonline.org/art-partnerships-community-resources-arts-education/

Kappan is the online journal for Phi Delta Kappan International. In print since 1916, it features articles on K–12 education including research and trends in teacher preparation, classroom instruction, curriculum design, assessment, education technology, student health and wellness, college transition, family and community engagement, and other topics.

www.communityartsla.com/

Community Arts Resources is a diverse collective of creatively minded planners and producers engaged in the changing dynamics of the urban environment in Los Angeles, CA. They partner with neighborhoods, nonprofits, cultural institutions, and designers to create public programs and events highlighting the uniqueness of a particular place. Sample projects can be found here, along with information on how to develop partnerships with nonprofits, city government, and so on.

apionline.org/

Art in the Public Interest is a clearinghouse for two major community arts publications no longer in publication: *High Performance Magazine* (published through 1997) and *Community Arts Network* (1999–2010). The archives of articles from these publications are available on this site. They provide many excellent examples of CBAE projects across the country.

www.nationalguild.org/

The mission of the National Guild for Community Arts Education is to provide opportunities for people of all ages to have outlets to maximize their creative potential. It is made up of institutional memberships with nonprofits, community arts organizations, and schools. They host professional development opportunities such as the Community Arts Education Leadership Institute (CAELI) and special interest groups such as ARE (Artists for Racial Equality), WARE (White Advocates for Racial Equality), Creative Aging Network, Creative Youth Development Network, and a host of others. Each year they hold a national conference for their members and artist-educators interested in networking.

www.swarthmore.edu/arts-social-change/websites

A listing of arts-based social change/social justice websites nationwide provided by Arts and Social Change at Swarthmore College.

https://www.swarthmore.edu/arts-social-change/annotated-bibliography-written-resources

An annotated bibliography of CBAE books provided by Arts and Social Change, Swarthmore College.

scholarscompass.vcu.edu/ijllae/

Founded by Pamela Harris Lawton, the *International Journal of Lifelong Learning in Art Education* (IJLLAE) is the official journal of the Lifelong Learning special interest group of the National Art Education Association (NAEA). IJLLAE seeks to provide a platform for researchers, educators, and artists working with populations both within and outside of formal K–16 art education. Particular interest is given to intergenerational arts learning and arts and aging programming.

www.fundsnetservices.com/

Funds Net Services is a fundraising and grants directory providing links to websites and brief descriptions of foundations and grantors for a variety of categories including arts and culture, education, social justice, and society.

www.awesomefoundation.org/en/about_us

The Awesome Foundation provides small grants ($1,000) for novel, experimental (awesome) projects in the arts, technology, community development, and more. Examples of past grantees are provided.

www.abladeofgrass.org/

A Blade of Grass is a fellowship program that provides resources and grants to artists working with communities for social change.

www.grants.gov/web/grants/search-grants.html

Grants.gov is a clearinghouse for searchable federal government grants by topic, such as "arts" and "community development."

www.artplaceamerica.org/

Artplace America is a 10-year collaboration (due to end in 2020) among a number of foundations, federal agencies, and financial institutions. This creative place-making site offers resources and examples of community projects and research.

www.artistcommunities.org/residencies

The Alliance of Artist Communities is an international association of artist residencies, listing over 1500 programs that support artists of any discipline in the development of new work.

roddenberryfoundation.org/

Founded in honor of *Star Trek* creator Gene Roddenberry, the Roddenberry Foundation provides three grant opportunities for social and environmental change.

imaginingamerica.org/

Imagining America is a consortium of colleges, universities, and cultural organizations bringing together scholars, artists, designers, humanists, and organizers to imagine, study, and enact a more just and liberatory America and world. Each year IA holds a conference through one of its member institutions. The website includes a blog and publications.

http://www.nationalartsstandards.org/sites/default/files/Media%20 Arts%20at%20a%20Glance%20-%20new%20copyright%20info.pdf

A downloadable PDF of the National Core Arts Standards for Media Arts for grades K–12.

https://www.nationalartsstandards.org/

A downloadable PDF of the National Core [Visual] Arts Standards for grades K–12.

CBAE Secondary Unit Plan by Samantha Strathearn

Unit Title: Community: Rural Spaces, Places, and People

SECTION 1. INTRODUCTION AND OVERVIEW

This unit plan is for a hypothetical high school art program or after-school art club in a small community that has the potential to visit community spaces on field trips. Led by the high school students, this unit will explore the relationship that community members have with the specific location in which the school resides, as well as the roles of various members in the community. It will also provide the opportunity for students to speak with people outside of their school, work to understand and be understood by people of different generations, and make art for and about the community in which they live. Students will be leaders in this project, and the unit will be designed to encourage questioning, idea generation, and collaboration. The artistic skills of this project relate to digital photography and filmmaking, but the lessons could be adapted to reach similar goals using low-tech processes (for example: painting/drawing/printmaking for portraits and land/cityscapes, illustrated statements, and texts/live readings for interviews).

Classroom Context

This unit is designed for an upper-level high school art class or art club. With greater supports for idea development, more structured activities, and some simplification, this unit could be adapted for a middle school group as well. I planned this unit for a group of students from a school located in a small rural town. This project would work best with at least 10 students in the class—workload and scope would be adjusted depending on the number of students in the class. This project will take place after students have had some basic DSLR camera training with manual functions. This unit also assumes that students can and will do homework, but if this is not possible, then the unit can be adjusted.

Technology

The artmaking in this unit is largely technology-based. Students will use DSLR cameras (or smartphones, iPads, or another form of photography equipment if these are not available), and video cameras (DSLR cameras if these are available). As the unit is written, there is a class set of DSLR cameras that students are able to take home with them. Students will also use video editing software on computers, as well as projectors to exhibit their final videos. To introduce artists, questions, and other information, I will use presentation software.

Time Allotted

Approximately 15 1-hour classes, and an exhibition night.

SECTION 2. RATIONALE

Students in upper-secondary art classes will likely be in the *Artistic Thinking* stage (Kerlavage in Simpson, et al., 1998)—where teens are entering adult thinking and gaining capacity for metacognition. They also have difficulty predicting or thinking about the results of their actions—students in this stage can be impulsive. Emotions can be sporadic. Students are also developing their sense of self in this stage. Physically, these students are in puberty, spanning from early to late stages. This unit works with students in this stage by allowing them to take leadership on larger projects, as they are more capable of adult thinking. This unit plans for confronting impulsivity because it requires students to plan their projects and interviews ahead of time, and to get feedback from their teacher and peers at various stages throughout the unit. Students are building interpersonal skills by initiating conversations with adults in their community, but also the unit addresses their discomfort with this by allowing them to plan, and to talk to them with a purpose in mind. In students' developing sense of self, this unit allows them to think deeply about their place in the classroom and larger community, as well as what connects them to the place in which they live. Students in this stage can use art as a creative process, and can use design carefully for expression. Students are engaged in the creative process throughout this unit. They will also carefully design their community portraits, landscapes/cityscapes, videos, and collaborative projects in order to highlight important aspects of their community. The unit expands upon students' real-world concerns and interests by exploring their community connections. This exploration is personal, and allows students to express their own ideas about their community and what they think is important both in community members and community spaces.

SECTION 3. BROAD GOALS

The broad goal of the unit is to explore the community and community roles of the place in which the school exists. Subthemes include exploring one's own community role, the importance of the community to other people, the role of place in community, how these parts fit together, and how art about the community can impact the community. This unit integrates social studies skills including interviews, local history, and community development.

National Visual Arts Standards (HS Accomplished)

Anchor Standard 1:
- VA: Cr1.1.IIa: Individually or collaboratively formulate new creative problems based on student's existing artwork.
- VA: Cr1.2.IIa: Choose from a range of materials and methods of traditional and contemporary artistic practices to plan works of art and design.

Anchor Standard 2:
- VA: Cr2.1.IIa: Through experimentation, practice, and persistence, demonstrate acquisition of skills and knowledge in a chosen art form.

Anchor Standard 3:
- VA: Cr3.1.IIa: Engage in constructive critique with peers, then reflect on, reengage, revise, and refine works of art and design in response to personal artistic vision.

NY State Visual Arts Standards

Students will:
- 1a: create a collection of artwork, in a variety of mediums, based on instructional assignments and individual and collective experiences to explore perceptions, ideas, and viewpoints
- 1b: create artworks in which they use and evaluate different kinds of mediums, subjects, themes, symbols, metaphors, and images
- 1c: demonstrate an increasing level of competence in using the elements and principles of art to create art works for public exhibition
- 1d: reflect on their developing work to determine the effectiveness of selected mediums and techniques for conveying meaning and adjust their decisions accordingly
- 2a: select and use mediums and processes that communicate intended meaning in their artworks, and exhibit competence in at least two mediums.
- 2b: use the computer and electronic media to express their visual ideas and demonstrate a variety of approaches to artistic creation

SECTION 4. UNDERSTANDING BY DESIGN—
SPECIFIC STUDENT OUTCOMES

Lesson 1:

Enduring understandings:
- A community is made up of the people that belong to it, connected to one another by common location, attitude, interest, or goals.
- Each person in a community has a role and is important in that community.

Essential questions:
- What does community mean?
- What is your role in your community?
- What keeps our community connected? What are our commonalities?

Objectives:
- Students will explore their community make-up and community roles through class discussions, and through the creation of a "mind map" that will be added to throughout the unit.
- Students will consider their own place in the community through individual visual journaling and written storytelling, and still-life photographs.

Lesson 2:

Enduring understandings:

- Communities based on location share common spaces.
- Places are connected to community collective memory.
- The physical community can show ideals of the community, as well as its past, present, and potential future

Essential questions:
- Each person in a community has a role and is important in that community.
- Community roles can change, and individuals can have multiple roles in a community.

Objectives:

- Students will work to understand their classroom community through interviewing one another, and through capturing portraits of their classmates.
- Students will work to understand the larger community to which their school belongs by brainstorming community roles and by interviewing and photographing community members.

Lesson 3:

Enduring understandings:

- Communities based on location share common spaces.
- Places are connected to community collective memory.
- The physical community can show the ideals of the community, as well as its past, present, and potential future.

Essential questions:

- How do communities connect to places and landmarks?
- What are important landmarks in our physical community?
- What about the physical location makes our community special and why?
- What places are important to you personally?
- Where are places in which the past is present in the physical community? The present?

Objectives:

- Students will explore the physical community through small- and whole-group discussions.
- Students will create photographic catalogs of landscapes/cityscapes of places in their community in order to document the locations that they find and their importance to the community.

Lesson 4:

Enduring understandings:

- A community is made up of individual people and places, and can be better understood through the examination of many elements.
- We can learn a lot about a community with careful examination.

Essential questions:

- How do community members relate to one another?
- What are commonalities among community members and places? What are the differences?
- How does hearing community stories help connect a community?

Objectives:

- Students will reflect upon what they learned about their community and their own roles in the community through the creation of a video about their community.

Lesson 5:

Enduring understandings:

- Art has the power to bring the community together.
- There is power in a community gathering.

Essential questions:

- How does creating artwork for, about, and with the community contribute to community relationships?
- How can we use art to bring the community together?
- What happens when a community gathers?

Objectives:

- Students will demonstrate appreciation for the community and exhibit their works about the community by hosting a reception and art show in a central community space.
- Students will work in small groups to design several collaborative and participatory projects for this event, demonstrating an understanding of the community and inquiry to learn more.
- Students will reflect on the project through writing artist statements, and through constructive critiques of one another's work.

SECTION 6. INSTRUCTIONAL STRATEGIES

See individual lesson plans.

SECTION 7. ASSESSMENT AND EVALUATION

Each project is graded on formative measurements: participation in discussion and planning, and individual writing prompts. Summative assessments consist of rubrics and student self-assessment sheets.

SECTION 8. RESOURCES AND BIBLIOGRAPHY

- Creative stages of development (Kerlavage, 1998)
- National Visual Arts Standards
- New York State Visual Arts Standards
- Judy Baca mural: www.judybaca.com/artist/portfolio/the-richmond-mural-project- the-extraordinary-ordinary-people/
- CNN photojournalists share their tricks: www.cnn.com/2011/IREPORT/09/02/capture.photo.bootcamp.irpt/
- Lily Yeh, *The Village of Arts and Humanities*

SECTION 5. CONTENT ANALYSIS

	Visual/ Spatial	Linguistic	Logical/ Math	Interpersonal	Intrapersonal	Kinesthetic	Naturalistic
Lesson 1	Looking at artwork	Group discussions, reading about an artist		Group painting, collaborative mind mapping	Journaling, considering own role in community	Large-scale painting	
Lesson 2	Looking at artwork	Group discussions, developing and conducting interviews		Interviewing	Individual writing		
Lesson 3		Group discussions			Individual writing	Taking a walk	Being outside, considering place
Lesson 4		Group discussions		Collaborative video-making	Individual writing		
Lesson 5	Looking at artwork	Group discussions	Matting and hanging artwork	Collaborative artmaking, exhibition	Reflective writing		

Principles of possibility (Gude, 2007) covered in this unit: Investigating community themes; reconstructing social spaces; attentive living; empowered experiencing; empowered making.

- Brandon Stanton, *Humans of New York*

SECTION 9. LESSON PLANS

Lesson 1: Exploring Community Roles

Time: 3 1-hour classes

Goal/Description: During this lesson, students will explore their community make-up and community roles. They will also work to discover their own place in their community, and express their ideas.

Big Ideas: Community roles

Objectives/Outcomes:

- Students will explore their community make-up and community roles through class discussions, and through the creation of a "mind map" that will be added to throughout the unit.
- Students will consider their own place in the community through individual visual journaling and written storytelling, and still-life photographs.

Enduring Understandings:

- A community is made up of the people who belong to it, connected to one another by common location, attitude, interest, or goals.
- Each person in a community has a role and is important in that community.

Essential Questions:

- What does community mean?
- What is your role in your community?
- What keeps our community connected? What are our commonalities?

Key Knowledge/Skills:

- Students will begin to practice collaborative idea development and artmaking through mind mapping and discussions about their community.
- Students will learn photography and design skills relating to lighting, subject matter, cropping, and angles.

Evaluation/Assessment:

- Still life: Rubric based on technical skills and idea development, student writing about planning, and how the final image relates to their role in the community in a self-assessment worksheet
- Participation in discussions and Sumi Ink Club activity [sumiinkclub. com/]—painting and sharing story
- Visual journal responses

Student Materials:

- Visual journals and writing utensils
- Sum ink, brushes, large roll of paper
- Mind map paper (approx. 3'x5') and markers
- DSLR cameras

Teacher Materials:

- Projector
- Judy Baca's *The Extraordinary Ordinary People*

Procedure:

Day One: Introducing Community

1. **Pre-assessment/Warm-up:**
   a. Bell ringer (independent writing): What does the word *community* mean? To what kinds of communities do you belong?
   b. After students have had time to think and write, they will contribute to a class mind map exploring the idea of community. The teacher and students will work together on a large sheet of paper to merge ideas together. One person will write at a time, and students will make connections to one another's ideas.
2. **Intro/Motivational Dialogue:**
   a. The teacher will explain that this unit will be using our community (that the school belongs to) as a theme, and designing works of art both collaboratively and individually for and about this community.
   b. Show students Judy Baca's community project from the Richmond (CA) Mural Project titled *The Extraordinary Ordinary People*, and read them the information about the project (or allow them to individually read) from the link below:
      i. www.judybaca.com/artist/portfolio/the-richmond-mural-project-the-extraordinary-ordinary-people/
   c. Ask students questions relating to *The Extraordinary Ordinary People:*
      i. Check for understanding: Who are the subjects of this process? How did Baca involve them in the process?

    ii. What does the title of this project mean?

    iii. What do we see in the panels? What items? How are portraits shown?

    iv. Relating to our own community: If we were to do a similar project, who would be the subjects of the artwork? What sort of stories might be told? What memorabilia might be included?

3. Demonstration/Introduction to Activity:

    a. First, students will work independently in their visual journals, answering the prompt, "Tell me a story about our community." Students will write this story down, and will know that it is a story that will be shared with the class.

    b. Students will use Sumi ink with soft paintbrushes of all different sizes. The teacher will demonstrate different brushes and qualities of the ink (how smoothly it applies to the paper, how quickly it dries, opaqueness, etc.).

4. Work Period:

    a. As a class, students will create a collaborative Sumi ink painting on a large roll of paper. The paper will be rolled out on a table, or several tables pushed together, so that each student has adequate space. More paper can be unrolled if students run out of room to work.

    b. Students will take turns reading their stories about community to the class. As each student reads, other students in the class will react to the story on the ink painting. Allow a few moments in between stories. The teacher will participate as well. The class should be silent except for the student talking.

    c. After the exercise is complete, ask students some questions: What themes did a lot of the stories have in common? What aspects of people's stories were unique? What did you learn about our community from the people in this class?

5. Cleanup:

    a. Students will wash paintbrushes and put them away. The mind map will be hung up where it can easily be referenced. If the Sumi painting is dry, it will be rolled up and stored for the exhibition.

6. Closure:

    a. Return to the mind map as a class. What else might we add to our community mind map after today's class? What were some common themes in our stories? What ideas did Baca's artwork inspire about community?

Day Two: Understanding Your Place in Community

1. Pre-assessment/Warm-up:

    a. Bell ringer (individual writing): Thinking back to our discussions about community last time, answer the following questions: Where do you fit into your community? How do you interact with the people in our town? What do you do to contribute through school? Through extracurricular activities? As a student/young person in general? Who are you connected to and why? Where do you feel like you don't fit within the community you live in?

    b. Pair share: Students will share their answers with a partner. Both partners will take turns telling, listening, and responding. They will also ask each other one clarifying question about their answers and their role in the community.

2. **Intro/Motivational Dialogue:**

    a. Let students know that we will focus on their own role in the community with the next assignment/project. We are all a part of the community in some way or another, and we will explore how we all fit in. Ask students to share with the class a few of their ideas about their community roles. What are similarities that many of us share? What are some ways in which you diverge from community expectations?

    b. Planning for still life: We will each create a digital photograph of a still life that explores your role in the community. Think about what this might show. It can be a collection of personal memorabilia (trophies, school objects, framed photos of community service on a desk, etc.). It might be a found collection of objects that represents your role (homework and a backpack, Boy Scout uniform hanging up, etc.). Consider the background, foreground, and middle ground.

    c. In their visual journals, students will plan their still lifes. This can be with words, sketches, or collages. They should have a good idea of what they might do before they leave class.

3. **Demonstration:**

    a. Still-life demonstration with DSLR cameras:

        i. Review camera manual functions.

        ii. Setting up a still life using viewfinders. Find focal points, balance, symmetry/asymmetry, color choice.

        iii. Considering angles: Try taking photos from below, higher up, eye-level, straight down, etc. How do the different angles affect the mood/meaning/idea behind your still life?

        iv. Lighting: Will you use natural lighting, dramatic artificial light, etc.? How will your lighting affect interpretation and meaning?

4. **Work Period:**

    a. Students will practice taking still lifes and composing photographs using the teacher's still-life objects. When they have had enough practice, they will continue to work on their plans for their own still lifes. They will also practice different camera settings.

5. **Cleanup:**

    a. Students will pack up their cameras and visual journals. The teacher's still-life objects will be put away.

6. Closure:
   a. For homework, students will take their still-life photographs using objects at home. (If it is not possible to take cameras home, then students will bring in photographs of their still life to school).
   b. Review what students discovered while practicing still-life photography.

Day Three: Editing and Reviewing Still Lifes

1. Pre-assessment/Warm-up:
   a. Bell ringer (individual writing): Choose three of your best still-life shots and upload them onto the computer. How do these shots express your role in the community? Why are these three your best photos?

2. Intro/Motivational Dialogue:
   a. This day is all about editing photos and considering meaning. Students will edit their three best shots, and choose which one they will turn in.

3. Demonstration:
   a. The teacher will demonstrate how to:
      i. correct and adjust white balances and exposure.
      ii. adjust color.
      iii. crop and straighten images.
      iv. turn an image into black and white if students want this.

4. Work Period:
   a. Students will edit their own photos, and the teacher will walk around and help students as needed. As students finish, they will work on a self-assessment worksheet about their still-life projects.

5. Cleanup:
   a. Students will hand in their printed photo, along with a self-assessment worksheet. They will save their digital photographs, and return the cameras and plug them in to charge.

6. Closure:
   a. Students will share their still-life photos with the class, or with a partner depending on the amount of time available when students are done working.

Plans for Differentiated Instruction:

- Written aspects of the lesson can be spoken out loud and recorded.
- Extra help can be given to students who need help with practicing still-life photography and editing.
- Helper students can be designated to assist students who are struggling with technical parts of the process.

Lesson 2: Stepping Outside Our Bubble: Reaching Out to Community Members

Time: 2 1-hour class periods. There should be adequate time between the two class periods to complete the interview project.

Goal/Description: During this lesson, students will continue to explore their community makeup and community roles, as well as reach out to community members to learn about the community from the community members themselves.

Big Ideas: Communities are made up of people

Objectives/Outcomes:

- Students will work to understand their classroom community through interviewing one another, and through capturing portraits of their classmates.
- Students will work to understand the larger community to which their school belongs by brainstorming community roles and by interviewing and photographing community members.

Enduring Understandings:

- Each person in a community has a role and is important in that community.
- Community roles can change, and individuals can have multiple roles in a community.

Essential Questions:

- Who are the "key members" and "local celebrities" of our community?
- What are important roles in the community, and how do they keep the town running?
- Who is important to you in this community personally?
- Who often goes unrecognized in the community?

Key Knowledge/Skills:

- Students will learn and practice a variety of digital photography portrait methods.
- Students will learn and practice using a DSLR camera to take videos.
- Students will practice emerging social and interpersonal skills by interviewing community members, and beginning to form relationships with people outside their school.

Evaluation/Assessment:

- Interviews: Consider questions asked; asked at least 8 questions of each person interviewed
- Portraiture of community member and of classmates: Rubric considering composition, subject matter, focus, edits, self-assessment worksheets

Student Materials:

- Access to "CNN Photojournalists Share Their Tricks" article: http://www.cnn.com/2011/IREPORT/09/02/capture.photo.bootcamp.irpt/
- DSLR cameras and tripods
- Visual journals
- Access to community members

Teacher Materials:

- Projector
- *Humans of New York* sample portrait with story
- DSLR camera and tripod

Procedure:

Day One:

1. **Pre-assessment/Warm-up:**
   a. *Humans of New York* bell ringer (individual writing): Looking at the example portrait of Brandon Stanton's *Humans of New York*, answer the following questions:
      i.   What is happening in this artwork?
      ii. What do you think about the person in the portrait based only on what you see?
      iii. How does the text express something about this person?
      iv. How does the portrait reflect the text?
   b. Discuss their answers as a whole group, and further explain *Humans of New York*.
2. **Intro/Motivational Dialogue:**
   a. Today, we are going to begin collecting portraits of the people in our community as well. If we were to do a similar project in our community, what might it look like?
   b. Explore community roles in small table groups, writing down answers:
      i. Who are the "key members" and "local celebrities" of our community?
      ii. What are important roles in the community, and how do they keep the town running?

        iii. Who is important to you in this community personally?
        iv. Who often goes unrecognized in the community?
  c. Talk about group answers as a class, while adding to the mind map from the first class.
  d. Each student will choose a specific person from the brainstorming session, or a few people, depending on the number of students in class and time available to complete the project. This is the person that they will interview for homework.

3. Demonstration:
  a. Students will read this article and flip through the slideshow on a computer, and then answer the questions below independently: "CNN Photojournalists Share Their Tricks," www.cnn.com/2011/IREPORT/09/02/capture.photo.bootcamp.irpt/
        i. What tips do you think will be helpful with portraiture? What tips might not be helpful?
  b. Teacher will demonstrate how a portrait might be set up, considering lighting (natural or artificial), background, distance from subject, subject pose, using a tripod, rule of thirds. Teacher will also talk about lens distortion with portraiture and encourage students to use a long lens to zoom in from a distance rather than a short lens.
  c. Teacher will demonstrate how to take a video on the DSLR camera, and let students know that getting a quality video of an interview is similar to taking a good portrait.

4. Work Period:
  a. During the work period, students will practice interviewing one another:
        i. First, they will develop a list of questions for the interview that investigates the person's role in the community, their memories of the place, their likes and dislikes, etc., such as, "Why do you live in this area?" or "What made you come to and stay in this area?"
        ii. Second, students will pair up with each other, and ask these questions of each other. The students will also video-record each other, and take some digital portraits of their classmates. They should first conduct the interview, and then consider how the person might best be captured based on what they learned about each other. The student should "take control" of the portrait subject, but also consider natural poses as well.

5. Cleanup:
  a. Students will save all digital files and then return all equipment to where it belongs.

6. Closure:

a. Individually, in their visual journals, students will write down answers to these questions regarding the interview that they conducted with a classmate:
   i. What did you learn about the person you interviewed in relation to their role in the community?
   ii. What more would you like to know?
   iii. How did your portrait of that person reflect what you learned about them from the interview?
   iv. How will you conduct your interview with a community member based on this experience?
b. Students may share any insights that might be helpful to the rest of the class as they prepare to work on this project outside of school.
c. The teacher will go over a few things about contacting a community member—how to politely ask them if they are interested in being interviewed for a project, how to contact them (by visiting their place of work if it's someone like a post office worker or storekeeper, or through their website, email, or phone number), reminding them to meet in a public place, unless that person is a family friend or safe person. (The teacher will prescreen all community members that students are considering talking to in order to make sure that students are safe. The teacher will also serve as a contact for more information about the project.)

Day Two:

1. **Pre-assessment/Warm-up:**
   a. Bell ringer (individual writing): What did you learn about the person you interviewed? What did they tell you about their community role that you didn't expect? What did you learn about your community based on what they told you?
   b. Share with a partner what you learned.
2. **Intro/Motivational Dialogue:**
   a. Today, students will be editing the photographs they took, and typing out the answers to their interview questions.
3. **Demonstration:**
   a. The teacher will review editing directions from Lesson 1.
4. **Work Period:**
   a. Students will work independently to edit their photographs. They will turn in their three best after they are edited.
   b. Students will fill out a self-assessment worksheet about their projects when they are done editing photos.
5. **Cleanup:**
   a. Students will return equipment and hand in their self-assessment, interview questions, and printed photos.

6. Closure:

a. Students will do a mini-critique of the photographs. Each student will put up one portrait photograph on the board. Students will use sticky notes to comment on one another's photographs, and provide feedback about how they see the portrait relating to the person's role in the community.

Plans for Differentiated Instruction:

- If students have difficulties with social interactions (such as anxiety, communication problems, etc.), they can work in pairs with other students, or can interview community members inside the school with the teacher there to help them if needed.
- Written work will not be graded on spelling and grammar, so students with difficulty in these areas will not be penalized. Written work can also be adjusted to include drawing, or dictating for someone else to write.

Lesson 3: Exploring Location and Place

Time: 2 1-hour class periods

Goal/Description: During this lesson, students will explore the places and landmarks that are important in the community, and personally important to the student. They will also work to discover connections between place and community development and cohesion.

Big Ideas: Communities share spaces

Objectives/Outcomes:

- Students will explore the physical community through small- and whole-group discussions.
- Students will create photographic catalogs of landscapes/cityscapes of places in their community in order to document the locations that they find are important to the community.

Enduring Understandings:

- Communities based on location share common spaces.
- Places are connected to community collective memory.
- The physical community can show ideals of the community, as well as its past, present, and potential future.

Essential Questions:

- How do communities connect to places and landmarks?
- What are important landmarks in our physical community?

- What about the physical location makes our community special, and why?
- What places are important to you personally?
- Where are places in which the past is present in the physical community? The present?

Key Knowledge/Skills:

- Students will learn and practice landscape/cityscape photography skills.
- Students will practice research skills related to local history.

Evaluation/Assessment:

- Landscape/cityscape: Rubric in regard to process, ideas, and composition, and self-assessment
- Research about location: check for understanding and accuracy

Student Materials:

- Access to the Internet and local history publications
- DSLR camera and tripod
- Computer to edit photos

Teacher Materials:

- DSLR camera and tripod
- Projector, local landscape artist (any medium) (In my community, there are several. One very well- known local artist is Gilbert Jordan, who does watercolor paintings in rural upstate New York.)

Procedure:

Day One:

1. **Pre-assessment/Warm-up:**
   a. Bell ringer (individual writing): Show the artwork of a local landscape artist, either living or deceased. If there is not a local artist who does landscapes, then historical photos of the local area will work as well. Questions:
      i. Do you recognize the place shown?
      ii. Why did the artist paint this?
      iii. How is this artwork meaningful to people who belong to our community? How might the meaning be different to someone outside our community?
2. **Intro/Motivational Dialogue:**
   a. Class discussion while working on the mind map:
      i. How do communities connect to places and landmarks?

>   **ii.** What are important landmarks in our physical community?
>   **iii.** What about the physical location makes our community special and why?
>   **iv.** What places are important to you personally?
>   **v.** Where are places in which the past is present in the physical community? The present?
>   **vi.** What kinds of places did the person you interview mention?

  b. Let students know the plan for the day: We will look for some of the locations that we discussed while on a walk outside with our cameras. Discuss expectations for going outside and taking a walk.

3. Demonstration:

  a. Once the group has walked to a location, the teacher will demonstrate, with and without a tripod, how to capture a landscape/cityscape using a wide lens. Consider capturing part of a place or a whole place. Consider capturing the scene with multiple photographs. Review angles and camera settings.

4. Work Period:

  a. Students will move from location to location as a group, and may take photos at any of the buildings that the group is near, as long as they do not go too far or go in the road. Each person will have a turn making suggestions about where to go next. If there is not a lot of the community within walking distance, then the students might consider capturing the school community during this work session.

5. Cleanup:

  a. Students will save files as necessary.

6. Closure:

  a. Discussion: What was your favorite place to photograph today? Where else would you like to go? The class will make a list of other places to go, and divide up the list among themselves, based on accessibility and interest to avoid duplication. If students would rather, they could also work in teams to capture all of the places on the list, and get together outside of school to do so. They will have leadership in this area. They will need to have the photographs for next class. Students will also take some video footage of their chosen places.

Day Two:

1. Pre-assessment/Warm-up:

  a. Bell ringer (individual writing): How did your photography assignment go? Where did you photograph, and what methods did you use?

2. Intro/Motivational Dialogue:

  a. During the introduction, students will spend some time researching the area that they photographed. They will use any publications available, as well as Internet sources. They will write a short description of their place, including history, and how they interpret it in the present day. Student writing will be used as descriptors in the final art exhibition.

3. Demonstration:
   a. Photo editing: The teacher will review photo editing software, as well as introduce some new features, including creative lighting filters.

4. Work Period:
   a. Students will edit their photos, and the teacher will help as needed and offer suggestions. About halfway through, the teacher will have students share their images with a partner sitting next to them for feedback.
   b. When students are finished, they will fill out their self-assessment worksheet.

5. Cleanup:
   a. Students will return all equipment and save all necessary files, and hand in photos.

6. Closure:
   a. Brief critique: Place all photographs on the table for students to see. Are we missing any place that we think is really important? What would you know about our community based on these images alone? Do they say what we want them to say?

Plans for Differentiated Instruction:

- Students have the option of working in teams. Within these teams, students can help each other with technical skills and other areas of assistance that might be needed.
- Students have choices about where they will photograph.

Lesson 4: Putting it All Together: Developing Video

Time: 1 day of instruction, and 2–4 days of video editing

Goal/Description: During this lesson, students will put all of their ideas and discovery about their community into one cohesive video. This lesson allows for student choice about how they will develop videos (individually, as a class, or in small groups), and how their videos will be structured.

Big Ideas: Community cohesion

Objectives/Outcomes:

- Students will reflect upon what they learned about their community and their own roles in the community through the creation of a video about their community.

Enduring Understandings:

- A community is made up of individual people and places, and can be better understood through the examination of many elements.
- We can learn a lot about a community with careful examination.

Essential Questions:

- How do community members relate to one another?
- What are commonalities amongst community members and places? What are differences?
- How does hearing community stories help connect a community?

Key Knowledge/Skills:

- Students will learn and practice video editing skills and how to combine each previous project into one cohesive video (either as a class or as individuals, depending on what students decide) by combining stills of the physical community, portraits, interviews, and their own voices.
- Students will practice storyboarding with their video projects, and creating timelines.
- If students choose to work in groups, they will practice collaboration and the give-and-take of working on an art project together.

Evaluation/Assessment:

- Participation in discussions
- Visual journals
- Video: Rubric—each student will have an individual grade based on their portion of the video if the students choose to work together. This will be arrived at with a rubric considering technical aspects, participation in the planning, ideas, and composition.

Student Materials:

- Video editing software
- Files from previous classes
- DSLR cameras and tripods
- Visual journals
- Video editing instruction packet

Teacher Materials:

- Projector and video editing software

Procedure:

Day One: Planning

1. **Pre-assessment/Warm-up:**
   a. Bell ringer (individual writing): What have you learned about your community so far that you didn't know before?
   b. As a class, add these answers to the community mind map. Find some common themes that we've all discovered over the previous lessons and exercises.
2. **Intro/Motivational Dialogue:**
   a. Let students know what we will be doing for the next few classes: We will be turning our video footage into cohesive videos about our community. This can be done by individuals with their own footage, small groups, or whole groups. Students will discuss what will work best. The teacher will make sure that no one is left out of groups. If students choose small groups, they will work with similar themes that they all discovered (like the community history or community values). They won't necessarily be in groups with their friends, and everyone will be included. If we work as a whole class, each person will have a section of the video to edit, and as a class we will develop a storyboard and timeline.
   b. Students will decide what route they want to take with this project. Some students might work on their own if they do not want to be a part of the larger group. Different requirements will be met for individuals versus groups (groups will have longer video requirements). Before the next step, they will take some time to assign themes and roles to the groups. If students work on their own, they will be allowed to overlap ideas and take it from their own perspective.
3. **Demonstration:**
   a. The teacher will demonstrate storyboarding. Each section of the student videos should have a panel in the storyboard. They will also plan music or voice-over for each section. Each video should include all of the assignments (stills from landscapes, portraiture, still-life, video of interview by student of community member, video from locations). There should also be titles, captions with people's names, location captions, and end credits. Students should have a script that ties all of the community ideas together, as well as their own perspectives.
   b. Students should also list additional footage that they might need to collect before they begin the process on the computers.
4. **Work Period:**
   a. Students will work on their storyboards, making sure that everyone's voices are heard if working in teams. Once they finish their

storyboards, they will check with the teacher about their ideas, to see if there is anything else they might have to research.

5. Cleanup:

    a. Hand in storyboards unless they need to finish outside of class.

6. Closure:

    a. In their visual journals, students will plan what they will need to accomplish during the next 2 to 3 days in class.

Day Two: Editing

1. Pre-assessment/Warm-up:

    a. Students will briefly share their plans with the class. If there are a few groups, then they will tell the whole class. If there are several individual video projects, then students will share at their tables.

2. Intro/Motivational Dialogue:

    a. Today we will be putting our videos all together using video editing software.

3. Demonstration:

    a. Video editing software: Demonstrate uploading video to timeline; trimming; moving videos and stills on timeline; slowing down and speeding up video; transitions; special effects; titles and text; and voice-over.

    b. Provide a packet with the directions as well.

4. Work Period:

    a. Students will work on their videos for the remainder of class, and the teacher will circulate through the room giving assistance. If students are working in teams, they will need to take time to assign roles and divide up the work.

5. Cleanup:

    a. Save all necessary files.

6. Closure:

    a. Progress report writing—What did you accomplish today? What needs to be done tomorrow? Who will work on what in the next days?

*Students will need more time to finish videos than this class—up to 4 days is likely. As they work, they will share at least 2 times with other groups/classmates for feedback.

Plans for Differentiated Instruction:

- Flexible grouping—students can work in teams or individually. The teacher can adjust groups to team up different skill levels as needed.
- Written work can be dictated and will not be graded on spelling or grammar.
- Flexible requirements—time length of final video can be adjusted and students can be provided with more work time if needed.

Lesson 5: Sharing with the Community

Time: At least 3 1-hour class periods, though likely more, and an exhibition night

Goal/Description: During this lesson, students will host a reception with the artworks and video in a central town space and invite the community to join them. Students will design collaborative projects that can take place at this event in which attendees and members of the community could participate. These projects will continue the documentary nature of the community unit and will be placed into a time capsule, alongside photographs and videos that the students created, for the community to rediscover at a later time.

Big Ideas: Bringing the community together

Objectives/Outcomes:

- Students will demonstrate appreciation for the community, and exhibit their works about the community by hosting a reception and art show in a central community space.
- Students will work in small groups to design several collaborative and participatory projects for this event, demonstrating an understanding of the community and inquiry to learn more.
- Students will reflect on the project through written artist statements and constructive critiques of each other's work.

Enduring Understandings:

- Art has the power to bring the community together.
- There is power in a community gathering.

Essential Questions:

- How does creating artwork for, about, and with the community contribute to community relationships?
- How can we use art to bring the community together?
- What happens when a community gathers?

Key Knowledge/Skills:

- Students will learn exhibition skills including preparing artwork for display, writing artist statements, navigating logistics (inviting people, announcements, etc.), and speaking to others about their work.
- Students will develop leadership and planning skills by creating a project for exhibit attendees to partake in and teaching participants how to participate in their project.

Evaluation/Assessment:

- Artist statements and self-assessment worksheets
- Group collaborative project: Rubric based on how it engaged the community; reflective writing about how it went, what they expected, and what they might do differently if they did it again.

Student Materials:

- Materials to hang artworks
- Miscellaneous materials for community collaborative project
- Materials for invitations, publicity (online and poster), and thank-you cards/gifts for community participants
- Some kind of storage device to use as a time capsule

Teacher Materials:

- Projector and artist images
- Community location to hang artwork and hold exhibition and reception that could last for several weeks—could be a local gallery if available, town hall space, library board room, etc. It would be helpful for this to be a short walking distance from the school.
- Projector and screen/blank wall to show videos

Procedure:

Day One:

1. **Pre-assessment/Warm-up:**
   a. Bell ringer (individual writing): How do you think all of our work from this unit might contribute to community relations? Do you feel like you are more a part of the community after doing these projects?
2. **Intro/Motivational Dialogue:**
   a. Introduce Lily Yeh's *The Village of Arts and Humanities*. Show her work first, and then tell the class her process.
   b. How did Lily Yeh impact this community? How did she involve them in the artistic process? How would you feel to be included in a similar project?
   c. Relating back to our own project: Review bell ringer answers.
   d. Tell students about the exhibition. We will be preparing three things: A collaborative art project in small groups to do at the exhibition, our artworks and artist statements for display, and publication materials to get people to our exhibition. Today we will be working in teams to make postcards/posters to spread around town, invitations for the people we interviewed and our families, an online publication, and thank-you cards for our participants.

3. Work Period:

    a. Students will work in teams to make these materials. They will first work as a class to decide on the information that is necessary to include—time, date, to be ready to make art and see artwork and videos, location, explanation of event, note if there will be food. Then they will design and mass-produce these items. Hand-drawn designs will be copied on a copy machine using nice paper. Invitations will be addressed personally and sent out.

4. Cleanup:

    a. Return all materials, clean up scraps, save all necessary files.

5. Closure:

    a. Share final products with the class. Assign students to distribute advertisement in different public locations.

Day Two:

1. Pre-assessment/Warm-up:

    a. Short discussion: Did anyone hear any news about who might come to our exhibition? Can the person you interviewed make it? Can your families? Can you? We might need to set up a carpool to make sure all students can make it.

2. Intro/Motivational Dialogue:

    a. Today, we will be designing projects that people can participate in during our exhibition, so they can learn even more about our community. Projects should ask some kind of prompt relating to community (e.g., Why is this place important to you? Why do you live here? What role do you play in the community?), and have an artmaking component. Some examples could be a guest book with a question to answer, a photo wall with participant photos and captions (Polaroid camera, digitally with a projector, quick printer), postcard artwork about community, sharing stories with a video camera. All of these projects, as well as our own, will be added to a community time capsule at the end of the exhibition.

    b. Brainstorm ideas and divide students into groups.

3. Work Period:

    a. Students will develop directions and create any instructional materials they need. They will also plan the process of how this will take place on the exhibition day.

4. Cleanup:

    a. Put away materials

5. Closure:

    a. Ask students if they are prepared, and if they need more time. Share ideas with class.

Day Three:

1. Pre-assessment/Warm-up:
   a. As a class, make a list of all of the projects from this unit on the board. We will work from this list as we prepare our artwork.

2. Intro/Motivational Dialogue:
   a. The last step is to hang our artwork for this exhibition. We will need to list materials to bring to our exhibition space, mat our 2D artwork, and prepare our video projects for viewing.

3. Demonstration:
   a. Matting demonstration
   b. Saving video projects to one location
   c. Placing and hanging artwork (will be done at exhibition space)
   d. Writing artist statements

4. Work Period:
   a. Students will work to complete all of the tasks in the demonstration.

5. Cleanup:
   a. At the exhibition space: Make sure everything is neat and tidy, artwork is straight on walls, etc.

6. Closure:
   a. Walk through exhibition space and enjoy their hard work.

Exhibition:

Students will attend the assigned exhibition night. They will direct their group collaborative projects, mingle with community members, and talk about and show their videos. They will also hand out thank-you cards/gifts to community member participants who were interviewed for the project. At the end of the evening, they will close the time capsule and present it to someone who will store it until the agreed-upon date of opening. The following class will include reflective writing about the experience, as well as a supportive critique of the exhibition before taking artwork down.

Plans for Differentiated Instruction:

- Flexible ability grouping
- Freedom to create a project that is interesting and within their capabilities

CBAE Elementary Unit Plan by Adjoa Burrowes

Unit Title: Brookland Community Collaborative Alphabet Book

SECTION 1. INTRODUCTION AND OVERVIEW

This unit provides 3rd-graders an opportunity to collectively explore the community where they live and go to school. In three lessons, students will create an alphabet book on the Brookland community by researching their neighborhood, writing informational text, and making prints. The finished book will be exhibited at the school and local library in Washington, DC. Prior to this unit, students have been studying identity and how various artists express identity in their art and explore a sense of place. The collaborative alphabet book flows naturally from that. After this unit, students will research artist's books and create their own with seniors in the community.

Classroom Context

This eager group of 3rd-graders lives in the Brookland community in the Northeast section of Washington, DC. Their class is comprised of primarily African American students; the second-largest ethnicity is Hispanic. Most students read below grade level, and a few have IEPs.

Technology

I will show students a PowerPoint in the beginning of the unit outlining the Alphabet Book project and show many examples of published informational alphabet books to show the range of what's out there. Students will research the Brookland community in the computer lab. I will ask a community photographer to videotape creation of the book in progress.

Time Allotted

The unit will take a total of 5 weeks to teach. The students will meet each week for a 45-minute session. The first lesson will take one session. Lesson 2 will take two sessions and Lesson 3 will take two sessions.

SECTION 2. RATIONALE

Students in 3rd grade are in the Symbol Making stage (7–9 years) and are more interested in the process than the final product. It is in this stage that children's art leans more toward realism in the expression of color and in the depiction of people. At this stage students may depict the importance of things by their size. This unit is valuable to children at this stage artistically because in 3rd grade students are still relatively uninhibited and love working in a variety of materials. Cognitively it is valuable because the unit calls for research and appeals to their sense of curiosity. Physically it is beneficial because it extends their fine motor skills as they write, draw, carve images in Styrofoam, and fold elements to construct the book manually. The unit will have a social-emotional appeal because it will allow them to work collaboratively and share their ideas. The unit relates to the real world because they are studying the world in which they live and go to school.

SECTION 3. BROAD GOALS

Goal: To foster a sense of pride and appreciation for the community

Theme: Community   Sub-theme: Identity

Academic Subject Matter: Reading/English Language Arts, Geography

National Visual Arts Standards

Content Standard 1: Understanding and applying media, techniques, and processes

Students use different media, techniques, and processes to communicate ideas, experiences, and stories

Content Standard 3: Choosing and evaluating a range of subject matter, symbols, and ideas

Students select and use subject matter, symbols, and ideas to communicate meaning

Content Standard 6: Making connections between visual arts and other disciplines

Students identify connections between the visual arts and other disciplines in the curriculum

DCPS Grade 3—Visual Arts Standards

3.2.10 Use a printing process to create an original work of art emphasizing rhythm and movement.

DCPS Grade 3—Geography of DC

3.1.3. Identify and locate major monuments and historical sites in and around Washington, DC.

3.1.4. Describe the various types of communities within the city (e.g., Chinatown, Foggy Bottom, Adams Morgan, Anacostia, and Georgetown), beginning with the community in which the elementary school is located. (G, S)

DCPS Grade 3—Reading/English Language Arts

3.W-E.3. Write up information on a topic that includes clear focus, ideas in sensible order, and sufficient supporting detail.

3.IT-E.2. Identify the facts given in a text

3.R.1. Identify and apply steps in conducting and reporting research.

Define the need for information and formulate open-ended research questions.

Initiate a plan for searching for information.

Locate resources.

Use and communicate the information.

3.IT-E.2. Identify the facts given in a text

3.W-E.3. Write up information on a topic that includes clear focus, ideas in sensible order, and sufficient supporting detail.

SECTION 4. UNDERSTANDING BY DESIGN— SPECIFIC STUDENT OUTCOMES

Students will be able to:

Brainstorm ideas individually and collectively; (**Explain**) Identify monuments and historical sites in the community; Research their community; (**Apply**) Initiate a plan for searching for information; Write informational text; (**Interpret**) Use and communicate information; Print illustrations; Work together to make an accordion book; Work collaboratively

Students will know:

The definition of a community; That communities are part of your identity; The role of text and illustrations in a book; What an alphabet book is; How to conduct research on a topic; Why artists work collaboratively; People, places and events in the Brookland community; How to use a journal; How to make an accordion book

Essential Questions

What makes a community? (**Self-Knowledge**) Is community a part of your identity? Why should people work collaboratively? How do you find out more information about a topic? What ways can you use to record your thoughts and information? What roles do art and text play in a book? What's the purpose of an alphabet book? Why would a person make a book about their community? (**Perspective**)

SECTION 6. INSTRUCTIONAL STRATEGIES

In Lesson 1 the teacher will give a PowerPoint presentation outlining the components of the book project and include samples of a variety of alphabet books. I will introduce the work of children's book author and illustrator Adjoa Burrowes and initiate discussion about what is a community. A whole group activity would include students viewing artwork from two of Burrowes's picture books and discussing differences and similarities between communities in the books and the Brookland community. Students will work on a word web to identify key words in their community. A second handout would allow students to identify more specific names of places in Brookland. We will discuss what else is needed and develop a plan to get more information.

In Lesson 2 students will look at a variety of alphabet books about Washington, DC, and compare and contrast them in groups. Students will be given a Brookland Scavenger Hunt handout to use in the computer lab to research people, landmarks, monuments, and historical places in the Brookland community. Back in the classroom, students will share what they have learned in their research. They will then choose a word relating to a person, place, or thing in the community and a corresponding letter that they would be responsible for writing text for. Sketch an illustration that represents their word.

In Lesson 3 students will write the informational text related to their chosen word and create another draft of the illustration for their page in the book. They will learn what a print is, create a picture, and print the image on their page. They will learn about accordion books and how one will house the student-created pages in the alphabet book. At the end of the lesson, we will have an Art Walk where the final accordion book will be displayed. The book will be displayed in the school library, and a reception for students, community and family members will be planned. The video created of the work in process will be shown. The book will then be exhibited at a library in the neighborhood.

SECTION 7. ASSESSMENT AND EVALUATION

Formative: Discussion and observation of picture books; process of creating prints, writing, accordion book; demonstrated understanding of research; how

SECTION 5. CONTENT ANALYSIS

Multiple Intelligences and Principles of Possibility Chart

	Visual/Spatial	Linguistic	Logical/Math	Interpersonal	Intrapersonal	Kinesthetic
Lesson 1	Creating artwork Empowered Making	Discussion/ critique of picture books Empowered Experiencing	Charting pre-assessment on board	Brainstorming ideas with a group Encountering difference	Small-group work discussions	
Lesson 2	Sketching in journal Forming Self	Writing journal entries Empowered Experiencing	Charting pre-assessment on board	Discussing picture books as a group Encountering difference		Creating a quick sketch in journal
Lesson 3	Sketching plan for book Creating illustrations Empowered Making	Interaction of text & image Discussing the work with the class	Charting pre-assessment on board	Writing and discussing words and illustrations Empowered Experiencing	Critiquing others installations	Creating an illustration Creating accordion book Gallery walk Empowered Making

students use the writing process and the elements and principles of design on their pages. Summative: Art Walk, class discussions, rubric.

SECTION 8. LESSON PLANS

See individual lessons.

SECTION 9. RESOURCES AND BIBLIOGRAPHY

Picture Books

Adjoa Burrowes, *Grandma's Purple Flowers*
Bryan Collier, *Uptown*
Sally Derby, *My Steps*
Ina Cumpiano, *Quinito's Neighborhood*
Dana Goldberg, *On My Block: Stories and Paintings by Fifteen Artists*
Eloise Greenfield, *Night on Neighborhood Street*
Quiara Alegria Hudes, *Welcome to My Neighborhood! A Barrio ABC*
Rachel Isadora, *Yo, Jo!*
Ezra Jack Keats, *Keats's Neighborhood: An Ezra Jack Keats Treasury*
Nancy I. Sanders, *An African American Alphabet: D is For Drinking Gourd*
Natasha Tarpley, *Destiny's Gift*
Carole Boston Weatherford, *Sugar Hill: Harlem's Historic Neighborhood*

ABC Books

John J. Feeley Jr. and Rosie Dempsey, *Brookland (Images of America)*
Muriel Feelings, *Jambo Means Hello: Swahili Alphabet Book*
Carla Golembe, *Washington, DC ABC's: An Alphabet Picture Book about Our Nation's Capital*
Quiara Alegria Hudes, *Welcome to My Neighborhood! A Barrio ABC*
Laura Krauss Melmed, *Capital! Washington D.C. from A to Z*
Nancy Sanders, *An African American Alphabet: D Is for Drinking Gourd*
Roland Smith and Marie Smith, *N is for Nations Capital: A Washington DC Alphabet*
Becky Williams, *Aiesha's Alphabet Book of Character*

Videos

Faith Ringgold, *Tar Beach*, www.youtube.com/watch?v=94tJtYXvML8

Websites

Brookland Community Development Corporation: www.brooklanddchistory.com/

"A fond look back at Brookland's history": www.washingtonpost.com/local/a-
     fond-look-back-through-brooklands- history/2011/09/28/gIQAT1Mn5K_
     story.html/
WAMU (2011): wamu.org/programs/metro_connection/11/09/23/door_to_
     door_crystal_city_va_and_brookland_dc/
Ghosts of DC: ghostsofdc.org/2013/02/06/map-of-brookland-in-1903/

Art/Integrated Lesson Plan–One

Title: Community   **Grade Level:** 3rd

Academic Subject: Reading/English Language Arts, Geography

Goal/Description: Students will explore what a community is and brainstorm
individually and in groups the key places, people and things in Brookland.

Developmental Rationale: Students in 3rd grade are in the Symbol Making
stage of artistic development (7–9 years). It is in this stage that children's art
leans more toward realism in the expression of color and in the depiction of
people, for example. At this stage students may depict the importance of things
by their size. This unit is valuable to children at this stage artistically because
3rd-grade students are still relatively uninhibited, yet seek to create realism in
their artwork; cognitively, because the unit calls for research; and physically,
because they will be using fine motor skills in the cutting, pasting, and folding
of elements to construct the book manually. In addition, the unit will have a
social appeal because it will allow them to work collaboratively.

Standards: DCPS Grade 3—Geography of DC

3.1.3. Identify and locate major monuments and historical sites in and around
     Washington, DC.
3.1.4. Describe the various types of communities within the city (e.g., China-
     town, Foggy Bottom, Adams Morgan, Anacostia, and Georgetown), begin-
     ning with the community in which the elementary school is located.

Big Ideas: Community is a part of one's identity. Communities can be different and the same.

Objectives/Outcomes: Students will define what a community is. Students
will identify key words associated with their community individually and in
groups. Students will compare and contrast their community with communities presented in children's books.

Enduring Understandings: Communities have people, places, and things that
make them unique. Words can help to define a community. Students can function as a community, working collaboratively toward a common goal.

Essential Questions:

- What does the word community mean?
- What makes a community?
- How is community a part of your identity?
- What roles do text and illustration play in a book?
- Why do artists work collaboratively?

Key Knowledge/Skills:

Declarative Knowledge: Brookland is a neighborhood in Washington, DC. Washington, DC is the capital city of the United States.

Procedural Knowledge: How to brainstorm and identify key words in the community. How to work together in a group. How to communicate ideas in large and small groups.

Evaluation/Assessment:

Formative: Pre-assessment chart on whiteboard, "My Brookland Community," with three headings (I know a lot about Brookland; I know a little about Brookland; I know almost nothing about Brookland). As students enter the classroom, they will be given a Post-it note and asked to put it in the column indicating how much they know about the Brookland community. To check for understanding along the way, we will have informal whole-group and small-group discussions.

Summative: At the end of this lesson, students will write three things they learned today about what makes a community in their journals.

Materials/Teacher Resources:

Supplies:

- White bond paper
- Pencils
- Large chart paper, Post-it notes, journals

Picture Books:

Adjoa Burrowes, *Grandma's Purple Flowers*
Sally Derby, *My Steps*
Eloise Greenfield, *Night on Neighborhood Street*
Quiara Alegria Hudes, *Welcome to My Neighborhood! A Barrio ABC*
Langston Hughes and Romare Bearden, *The Block*
Rachel Isadora, *Yo, Jo!*
Ezra Jack Keats, *Keats's Neighborhood: An Ezra Jack Keats Treasury*
Natasha Tarpley, *Destiny's Gift*

Carole Boston Weatherford, *Sugar Hill: Harlem's Historic Neighborhood*

Websites

Brookland Community Development Corporation: www.brooklanddchistory.com/
"A fond look back through Brookland's history": www.washingtonpost.com/local/a-fond-look-back-through-brooklands- history/2011/09/28/gIQA-T1Mn5K_story.html/
WAMU (2011): wamu.org/programs/metro_connection/11/09/23/door_to_door_crystal_city_va_and_brookland_dc/
http://ghostsofdc.org/2013/02/06/map-of-brookland-in-1903/

Videos

Faith Ringgold, *Tar Beach*, www.youtube.com/watch?v=94tJtYXvML8

Teaching Procedure/Time Allotted: 45 minutes

Pre-assessment:

Pre-assessment chart on the board, "My Brookland Community," with three headings (I know a <u>lot</u> about Brookland; I know a <u>little</u> about Brookland; I know <u>nothing</u> about Brookland). As students enter the classroom, they will be given a Post-it note and asked to put it in the column indicating how much they know about the Brookland community before they sit down.

Intro/Motivational Dialogue:

What is a community? Is it the same as a neighborhood? If so, why or why not? Is the Brookland community unique? If so, in what ways? Why or why not?

Demonstration:

PowerPoint outlining the components of the book project.

Look at the artwork in the children's books *Destiny's Gift* by Natasha Tarpley and *My Steps* by Sally Derby, both illustrated by Adjoa Burrowes. What's going on in these pictures? What makes you say that? Are these communities? How are these communities different from Brookland? In what ways are they the same? View the *Tar Beach* video. Discuss her interpretation of community.

Pass out Handout #1, *Brookland Community Word Web*. Students write individually all the words that come to mind when they think of the Brookland community.

Students then work in groups of 4 to discuss their findings. One student will act as recorder and list all words on a large sheet of paper, being careful not to duplicate words. The sheets of paper will be taped onto the whiteboard in front of the class.

Whole-group discussion: A student will report to the class from each group while standing in front of their large sheet.

Pass out Handout #2, *What's in the Brookland Community*. Students will pair off and list *specific* names of monuments, parks, churches, stores, sports teams, other schools, and so on in Brookland. In whole class, develop a plan to get missing information.

Work Period: 45 minutes

Cleanup:

Closure:

Students will write 3 new things they learned about the Brookland community today in their journals. While standing in line to exit classroom, each student will say one thing they learned.

Plans for Differentiating Instruction

Students can help one another brainstorm and write while working in groups.

Teacher Reflection

This lesson involves mainly writing and discussion. However, the students will be engaged as they brainstorm words and discuss what a community is, in both pairs and small groups.

Art/Integrated Lesson Plan–Two

Title: ABC Books   Grade Level: 3rd

Academic Subject: Reading/English Language Arts, Geography

Goal/Description: Students will study ABC books and do research for a collaborative alphabet book that explores the Brookland community in northeast Washington, DC.

Developmental Rationale: Students in 3rd grade are in the Symbol Making stage of artistic development (7–9 years). It is in this stage that children's art leans more toward realism in the expression of color and in the depiction of people, for example. At this stage students may depict the importance of things by their size. This unit is valuable to children at this stage artistically because in 3rd grade students are still relatively uninhibited, yet seek to create realism in their artwork; cognitively, because the unit calls for research; and physically, because they will be using fine motor skills in the cutting, pasting, and folding of elements to construct the book manually. In addition, the unit will have a social appeal because it will allow them to work collaboratively.

Standards: DCPS Grade 3—Reading/English Language Arts

3.R.1. Identify and apply steps in conducting and reporting research. Define the need for information and formulate open-ended research questions. Initiate a plan for searching for information. Locate resources. Use and communicate the information.

Big Ideas: Appreciating the history and culture of our community.

Objectives/Outcomes: Students will conduct research on the Internet to gather more specific information about people, places, and events in the Brookland community. Students will look at a variety of informational ABC books and discuss similarities and differences and what makes them unique.

Enduring Understandings: By researching a topic, you can gain valuable information. You can learn by talking with people in the community.

Essential Questions:

- How do you gather more information about a topic?
- What is a key word?
- How do you record your information?

Key Knowledge/Skills:

Declarative Knowledge: A community is made up of many people, places, and things. You can use technology to find information.

Procedural Knowledge: How to conduct research on the Internet. How to use a journal to write notes. How to present what you learned to a group.

Evaluation/Assessment:

Formative: To check for understanding along the way, we will have informal whole-group and small-group discussions.

Summative: At the end of this lesson, students will write three NEW things they learned today about Brookland as a result of their research.

Materials/Teacher Resources:

Supplies:

- White bond paper
- Pencils
- Large chart paper
- Journals

Picture Books

Muriel Feelings, *Jambo Means Hello: Swahili Alphabet Book*

Carla Golembe, *Washington, DC ABC's: An Alphabet Picture Book about Our Nation's Capital*
Quiara Alegria Hudes, *Welcome to My Neighborhood! A Barrio ABC*
Laura Krauss Melmed, *Capital! Washington D.C. from A to Z*
Nancy I. Sanders, *An African American Alphabet: D Is for Drinking Gourd*
Marie and Roland Smith, *N is for Our Nation's Capital: A Washington DC Alphabet*
Becky Williams, *Aiesha's Alphabet Book of Character*

Teaching Procedure/Time Allotted: 45 minutes

Pre-assessment:

Find out what students know about ABC books. Document how they respond to guide your teaching. (Note their knowledge, questions, what they leave out, and confusions.)

Intro/Motivational Dialogue:

What's the purpose of alphabet books? Why do we need to research something? What are some things we could find out about Brookland by doing research?

Demonstration:

Introduce class guest: local photographer and how he/she will be working with our class.

Look at a variety of informational alphabet books about Washington, DC. Pass out a different alphabet book to each group and Handout #3, *Washington, DC ABC Books*, to each group of four students. Discuss questions on the handout in the groups. One student in each group will report their answers back to the whole class.

Pass out Handout #4, *Brookland Scavenger Hunt*, to use in the computer lab. Pass out journals for students to take also. Go over instructions for computer lab.

In the computer lab, students will go to selected websites to find answers to questions on the handout and write answers in their journals. On return to the classroom, students will get back in their groups and one person will compile all answers from the group on a single sheet, being careful not to duplicate.

Teacher will write the alphabet on the whiteboard. As teachers call out letters from A to Z, students in any group can share a word that begins with that letter. Teacher will write it on board. Afterward we will be able to see which letters are lacking. As a group we will brainstorm solutions.

One at a time, students will choose a single letter with its word until every student has one. Teacher will discuss how artists visualize. Students will write their word and letter in their journal and draw pencil sketches of ideas to illustrate it.

Work Period: Two 45-minute sessions

Clean-Up: none

Closure:

Students will write one new thing they learned about the Brookland community today and one thing they felt was challenging when they did their research in their journals. While standing in line to exit classroom, each student will contribute one thing they learned.

Plans for Differentiating Instruction:

Students can help one another brainstorm and write while working in groups. Teacher can work one-on-one with students who may have challenges working with the computer.

Teacher Reflection:

This lesson should engage students in critical thinking and dialogue while working in small groups and participating in whole-class discussions as well as conducting research on the Internet.

Art/Integrated Lesson Plan—Three

Title: Making Prints   Grade Level: 3rd

Academic Subject: Reading/English Language Arts, Geography

Goal/Description: Students will write and make prints for a collaborative alphabet book that explores the Brookland community in northeast Washington, DC.

Developmental Rationale: Students in 3rd grade are in the Symbol Making stage of artistic development (7–9 years). It is in this stage that children's art leans more toward realism in the expression of color and in the depiction of people, for example. At this stage students may depict the importance of things by their size. This unit is valuable to children at this stage artistically because in 3rd grade students are still relatively uninhibited, yet seek to create realism in their artwork; cognitively, because the unit calls for research; and physically, because they will be using fine motor skills in the cutting, pasting, and folding of elements to construct the book manually. In addition, the unit will have a social appeal because it will allow them to work collaboratively.

Standards:

DCPS Grade 3—Visual Arts Standards

3.2.10 Use a printing process to create an original work of art emphasizing rhythm and movement.

DCPS Grade 3—Reading/English Language Arts

3.W-E.3. Write up information on a topic that includes clear focus, ideas in sensible order, and sufficient supporting detail.

Big Ideas: Text and images must work together in a picture book. Pictures communicate information just like text.

Objectives/Outcomes: Students will write text in relation to their selected letter of the alphabet. Students will create an illustration that goes along with their text.

Enduring Understandings: Artists sometimes work with text and images. The Elements of Art and Principles of Design can be used to create illustrations.

Essential Questions:

- What is the purpose of illustrations in a book?
- Why make a book about a community?

Key Knowledge/Skills:

Declarative Knowledge: A picture book can have both pictures and text. An alphabet book presents information and pictures about letters from A to Z and is usually based on a theme.

Procedural Knowledge: How to create an illustration for a book. How to write words and sentences for an alphabet book. How to construct an accordion-fold book.

Evaluation/Assessment:

Formative: To check for understanding along the way, we will have informal whole-group and small-group discussions.

Summative: At the end of this lesson students will write three NEW things they learned today about Brookland as a result of their research.

Materials/Teacher Resources:

Supplies

- White bond paper, lined writing paper, pencils
- Scissors
- Glue sticks
- Large chart paper
- Journal
- Styrofoam plates
- Rollers
- Water-based ink
- Newspapers

Picture Books

Muriel Feelings, *Jambo Means Hello: Swahili* Alphabet *Book*
Carla Golembe, *Washington, DC ABC's: An Alphabet Picture Book about Our
    Nation's Capital*
Quiara Alegria Hudes, *Welcome to My Neighborhood! A Barrio ABC*
Laura Krauss Melmed, *Capital! Washington D.C. from A to Z*
Nancy I. Sanders, *An African American Alphabet: D Is for Drinking Gourd*
Marie and Roland Smith, *N is for Nation's Capital: A Washington DC Alphabet*
Becky Williams, *Aiesha's Alphabet Book of Character*

Teaching Procedure/Time Allotted:

Pre-assessment:

Teacher will have 3 boxes on a front table in my classroom. One box will be labeled "I <u>have</u> made my own book before"; a second one will be labeled "I <u>wish</u> I
could make my own book"; and a third box will be labeled "I've <u>never</u> made a
book before." As students enter the classroom, they will be given a color ticket
and instructed to place the ticket in the appropriate box. After the students sit
down, I will tally the results and note the numbers on the board.

Intro/Motivational Dialogue:

What ABC books do you remember from when you were little? What did you
like about them?

Demonstration:

Teacher will demonstrate the structure of the accordion book, step by step, and
talk about the components beginning with the writing of text. Teacher will
model writing the text.

Teacher will pass out rubric and discuss Handout #5, *Rubric for Alphabet
Page.*

Students will write down their specific letter and word and begin writing
text describing the words *community connection*. Teacher will model. Students
will write first draft.

In small groups of four, students will read their text to the group for critique. Students will offer feedback. A second draft is made. Teacher will edit,
and a final version is written on paper to be pasted on a page later.

Teacher will model how to make a print using Styrofoam plates.

Students will sketch their picture ideas in their journal and then discuss
their choice in their small groups. Students will draw on the Styrofoam plates
and then print it on paper.

Students will draw the alphabet letter in the right corner and then add the
text using markers. Teacher will model.

Students will fold the accordion book form with the art and text pages when they are dried. After completion, there will be a Gallery Walk to view the final collaborative book.

Work Period: Two 45-minute sessions

Cleanup: Wash rollers. Clean up tables.

Closure:

Students will write 3 new things they learned about the bookmaking process in their journals. 2–4 students will be picked to verbally contribute one thing they learned.

Plans for Differentiating Instruction:

Students can help one another write while working in groups and help come up with picture ideas. I can work one-on-one with students who may have challenges printing.

Teacher Reflection:

This lesson should be engaging as students write, create prints, and participate in small-group and whole-class discussions.

MY BROOKLAND COMMUNITY

I know a lot about Brookland	I know a little about Brookland	I know nothing about Brookland

This represents a large chart that will be drawn on the board for pre-assessment on Day 1. Students will place Post-it notes indicating how much they know about Brookland.

BROOKLAND COMMUNITY WORD WEB

Write down as many words as you can think of about Brookland.

WHAT'S IN THE BROOKLAND COMMUNITY

Grocery Stores in Brookland	Churches in Brookland	Sports Teams in Brookland
Monuments in Brookland	Schools in Brookland	Historical Sites in Brookland
Streets in Brookland	Jobs in Brookland	Restaurants in Brookland

Other people, places or things in Brookland:

WASHINGTON, DC ABC BOOKS

- Write the title of your book.
- What do you notice about your book?
- What do you notice about the pictures?
- What do you notice about the writing? What is your ABC book about?
- Does the book make you wonder about anything?

BROOKLAND SCAVENGER HUNT

- Find the names of two churches in the community.
- Find the names of two recreational centers.
- Find the names of two famous people who used to live in Brookland.
- Find the names of two major streets in Brookland.
- What ward is Brookland in?
- What universities are in Brookland?
- What former President had a cottage in Brookland?

RUBRIC FOR MY ALPHABET PAGE

	Fantastic!	Good	Could Use Improvement
Writing	I wrote using description and spelled everything correctly. My punctuation was great.	I spelled everything right, and most of my punctuation was right.	I had several misspelled words and the punctuation was not correct.
Research	I did a great job researching my topic and included facts in my writing.	I included only 1 fact about my topic.	I didn't research my topic.
Art	I created a great picture. It was original and worked well with my text.	My picture matched my text a little.	My picture didn't match my text.
Printing	I printed my picture neatly on the page. No fingerprints.	My picture was printed somewhat neatly on my page. Some fingerprints.	My picture was sloppy on the page. A lot of fingerprints.
Page Elements	I included my alphabet letter, my picture, and text on my page.	One element was missing on the page.	I only included one element on my page.

CBAE Proposal by Erin McArdle

A *NOVEL* DIGITAL NARRATIVE PROJECT

When studying novels in my high school English class, students typically read assigned chapters for homework, and in class, discuss key ideas, themes, and stylistic development. At the end of the study, students have a written assessment on class discussions and readings. As an extension, after a novel is finished, I usually have students complete some type of writing project, such as a research paper, speech, or argument essay. For this novel, this digital narrative will be our final project. This type of culminating project will lend itself well to the study of the novel because one of the main areas of study while we read is the development of the narrative, which acts as a model for students for their own projects. The inclusion of photographs and other visuals also acts as a model for how students can effectively incorporate visuals into their digital narratives.

I will use this project as a culminating activity after we read the novel *Extremely Loud and Incredibly Close* (2005) by Jonathan Safran Foer. After students have read the novel, participated in class discussions and activities about the novel, and completed an assessment, students will be first given a written assignment for the initial aspect of their digital narrative. A well-planned written narrative is the first step to creating a digital narrative. Since the story will, at first, be based on only one photograph, students will focus on the narrative behind the story in this part of the design process. Students will complete this written narrative at home, and bring it to class with the accompanying photograph on the assigned due date.

Once students complete their written narrative, they will then begin to work collaboratively with other students to develop their ideas. I will assign each student to a peer review partner to ensure that students confer with a student who can benefit him or her in some aspect. For example, if I know one student struggles creatively, I will pair him with a student who has creative ideas. Or if a student struggles with his stylistic complexity, I will pair him with a student who is stylistically advanced. Students will participate in a peer review activity in class while I individually conference with students. I will read through their writing, offer my feedback, and direct students to complete a more comprehensive version of their first draft. By doing this in the early stages, I will have a good understanding of expected progression.

After students have individually conferenced with me and have participated in a peer review activity, students will be directed to create a final draft for submission. I will assess each narrative and provide students with individual, written feedback on their narrative. I will also make suggestions to students on how they can transform this written narrative into a digital narrative. After students receive their written narratives and feedback, students will write a brief reflection on their completion of the first half of their project. Students will be directed to reflect on their ideas and narrative flow and will be asked to postulate how they could turn this into a digital representation.

After students reflect on their written narrative, students will then be introduced to the genre of digital storytelling and will partake in critical analysis by viewing and discussing three digital narratives. After we view them as a class, I plan on discussing the images the creator chose to use, music, and pacing of the voiceover. I also plan on discussing the connections students made to the narrative. Could they draw any parallels to their own lives? This will start to develop a sense of classroom community, since they are viewing others' stories and making personal connections.

Following a discussion of the models, we will move into production mode. Students will be given instructions for their digital narrative, which we will discuss as a class. Students will first be directed to complete a digital narrative script template. Students will complete this outside of class for homework. Then students will participate in a writing workshop in class. Here, they will share ideas and get feedback from their peers about their stories.

Next, students will be directed to record the audio for their digital narratives. This will be done at home in order to provide a quiet space to record. Students who do not have access to recording devices outlined in the directions will be provided audio recording equipment by the school (which I will attain for students if they need it).

After students record their audio at home, I will arrange for students to use iMovie in the computer lab at school. First, students will be directed to bring in 8–10 digital images and a music file that they can use to enhance their digital narratives. I will arrange for the media center specialist to give students a tutorial on iMovie, which all students can access at school and at home through signing onto our school's server. Students will be given two to three class periods to work with iMovie and create their narratives.

After students have finished the rough draft of their narratives, they will be assigned to a group of four students. Each person will play his or her narrative for the group, and the members will provide feedback. Students will then be given the opportunity to edit their narratives for final publication. After all students have a final product, I will ask for a small group of students to volunteer to organize the stories into one final project. I would suggest that these students create an introductory set of graphics that unifies the class as a community and includes everyone's names. I would also advise the group to create some sort of sequential organizational pattern, such as by theme, ideas, or effects. I would also instruct the students to create a closing where they unify the stories with some quotations, final photographs, or a group picture of the entire class. After they complete the project, we will view it as a class and discuss what we have learned.

My objectives for the class viewing and discussion will be to unify us as a class community. Although I cannot exactly predict the outcome, I can foresee that some students may have thematically similar ideas or story basis. My class discussion questions would lead students to make connections that transcend gender, race, religion, age, and ethnicity. I will ask leading questions so that students can come to recognize our commonalities. By doing this, I hope students will break down their barriers and be more likely to make connections with their peers whom they once viewed as an "other." After the discussion, I will have students reflect on the process.

Students will complete their Personal Reflections to think about not only the digital writing process, but also how the digital narratives linked us as a class community.

After we complete the project, I will have our school media center publish the class narrative on appropriate venues where other students, faculty, and parents can view it. I foresee that appropriate venues for this project would be our school's website, our school's Facebook and Twitter pages, and my teacher website.

CONCLUSION

In order to ensure success of this project, I, as the instructor, need to make time for careful reflection and questioning techniques as we progress through the project. The final project, the string of digital narratives, will meet my objective of uniting my classroom community only if we allow for significant discussion and contemplation. My students must make connections with their peers in order to develop a sense of classroom community—something that unifies and links them together.

Worksheets for Assignment

Personal Narrative Rubric

Stimulating Ideas   1   2   3   4   5

Focuses on a specific event or experience
Presents an engaging picture of the action and people involved
Contains specific details and (potentially) dialogue

Makes readers want to know what happens next
Includes a copy of the photograph

Logical Organization   1   2   3   4   5

Includes a clear beginning that pulls readers into the essay
Presents ideas in an organized manner
Uses transitions to link sentences and paragraphs
Flows smoothly from one idea to the next

Engaging Voice   1   2   3   4   5

Speaks knowledgably and/or enthusiastically
Shows that the writer is truly interested in the subject
Contains specific nouns, vivid verbs, and colorful modifiers

Grammar/Conventions   1   2   3   4   5

Sentence structure and variety
Spelling, punctuation, capitalization
Word choice and usage
No typos or other errors

Attention to Directions   1   2   3   4   5

2–3 pages in length
Used an interesting font or way of presenting the written word
Included a cover page

Each section is worth 10 points   FINAL GRADE: _______/50

STUFF THAT HAPPENED TO ME: A MULTIMODAL PERSONAL ESSAY, THE SPRINGBOARD FOR YOUR DIGITAL NARRATIVE

Background:

Jonathan Safran Foer includes visual material in his novel because he believes our memory of events, such as the terrorist attack on the World Trade Center, are experienced in images (Koster, 2011).

Foer relates his use of images to the experience of national trauma and at the same time highlights the influence of images on the construction of a collective memory when he claims that an event is remembered by its images. Oskar's narrative includes graphic images that originate from his visual diary called "Stuff That Happened to Me." Oskar collects all kinds of images that document his daily experiences and help him to express what he cannot put into words. In this modern world, pictures and images do truly "say a thousand words."

Assignment:

You will:

Choose a photograph (<u>not</u> a painting, sculpture, watercolor, etc.) that you think represents something significant about yourself. It can be a personal photograph, but doesn't have to be.

Create a connection to one of the themes developed in *Extremely Loud and Incredibly Close* (death, loss, family, coming-of-age, etc.)

Compose a 2–3-page personal narrative that *puts the picture into words.*

Special Instructions:

Please be creative with text and color to help support your purpose.

SPECIFICATIONS OF A PERSONAL NARRATIVE

Purpose and Audience

Personal narratives allow you to share your life with others so they can vicariously experience the things that happen around you. Your job as a writer is to put the reader in the midst of the action, letting him or her live through an experience. Although a great deal of writing has a thesis, stories are different. A good story creates a dramatic effect, makes us laugh, gives us pleasurable fright, and/or gets us on the edge of our seats. A story has done its job if we can say, "Yes, that captures what living with my father feels like," or "Yes, that's what being cut from the football team felt like."

Structure

There are a variety of ways to structure your narrative story. The three most common structures are: chronological approach, flashback sequence, and reflective mode. Select one that best fits the story you are telling.

Methods

Don't tell the reader what he or she is supposed to think or feel. Let the reader see, hear, smell, feel, and taste the experience directly, and let the sensory experiences lead him or her to your intended thought or feeling. Showing is harder than telling. It's easier to say, "It was incredibly funny," than to write something that is incredibly funny. The rule of "show, don't tell" means that your job as a storyteller is not to interpret; it's to select revealing details. You're a sifter, not an explainer. <u>An easy way to accomplish showing and not telling is to avoid the use of "to be" verbs</u>. Try to use figurative language in your writing. We will talk about this more after you complete your rough draft.

Let People Talk

It's amazing how much we learn about people from what they say. One way to achieve this is through carefully constructed dialogue. Work to create dialogue that allows the characters' personalities and voices to emerge through unique word selection and the use of active rather than passive voice. <u>Although using dialogue can be effective, it is not required that you include it in your narrative.</u>

Choose a Point of View

Point of view is the perspective from which your story is told. It encompasses where you are in time, how much you view the experience emotionally (your tone), and how much you allow yourself into the minds of the characters. Most personal narratives are told from the first-person limited point of view. If you venture to experiment with other points of view, you may want to discuss them with Mrs. McArdle as you plan your piece.

Tense

Tense is determined by the structure you select for your narrative. Consider how present vs. past tense might influence your message and the overall tone of your piece.

Tone

The tone of your narrative should set up an overall feeling. Look over the subject that you are presenting and think of what you are trying to get across. How do you want your audience to feel when they finish your piece? Careful word choice can help achieve the appropriate effect.

Peer Review: "Stuff That Happened to Me"

Reviewer: _______________________________________

Read the draft carefully at least <u>twice</u>. Complete the following questions:

- Write down your overall impression of the essay.
- Summarize what you think is the writer's main point.
- What major concerns do you have about the piece (questions that you had as you read, parts you'd like to know more about, etc.)?
- How does the essay prompt you to think differently?

- What details could be elaborated upon to illustrate the main idea? Note instances where the writer could provide details to *show* rather than *tell*.
- Does the climax of the story have enough detail to make that the most important event in the story?
- Highlight/underline any details that seem unrelated to the main idea.
- Is there dialogue that is relevant to the story? If not, mark where there could be dialogue to add to the richness of the story.
- Is the dialogue punctuated correctly?
- Are the paragraphs coherent? Does the essay seem organized in a specific order? If not, what do you recommend?
- How does the essay begin? Is that as exciting and intense as it could be? What would you recommend?
- Do you think the writer has effectively used a photograph to help support his or her narrative? Why or why not?
- List the characters of the story here and write a sentence or two of description. If you cannot describe the characters (personality and/or physical description as appropriate), what recommendations do you have for the author?
- Mark any spelling, punctuation, or grammar errors before giving the piece back to the author. You don't need to make corrections—just circle errors.

Digital Narrative

Objective: Learners will create a 3–4-minute digital video clip, told in first-person narrative [*begins with a written script based on their narrative essays*], told in their own voice [*record script with student's own voiceover*], illustrated (mostly) by still images and personal photographs, and with a music track to add to an emotional tone. Students will then form one continuous class narrative that will be viewed by the class, and participate in a class discussion on how we came together as a community to create this class digital narrative.

1. Write a script for your story and get feedback

Use the script template (attached below) that I have provided, answering these questions: Who is your audience? What is your dramatic question? You may want to go over your script with a facilitator or another person before recording your voiceovers. In hands-on workshops, we spend some time sharing the stories in a group process called a "story circle."

Keep your story to less than 400 words, which works out to about a page of single-spaced text. One of the video clips that you watched talks about the seven elements of digital storytelling. One of these, economy, emphasizes the simplicity of digital stories: where you have images, you may not need narrative explanation. Think of your story as a multimedia sonnet, with characteristics of poetry. Use the script template to identify the images that you will want to match with your narration. Or consider using Google Docs or any wiki for collaborative or group story writing and editing.

2. Create a digital audio clip of your story

You will need to use a microphone to record your story. There are several types of microphones:

1. Microphone built into laptop computers (only use if you have nothing else)
2. USB microphone
3. Standard computer microphone that plugs into a microphone port or sound card
4. iPod with microphone
5. Digital audio recorder

When you are ready to record your script, find a quiet place to record. Surprisingly, a great place to record audio is in a walk-in closet with lots of clothes (the clothes deaden the noise). Record only short sections of your story at one time. You can pause recording in a single file, or record separate clips, which you should name as sequentially numbered files. You might use the script template to write down the names of the files, if they are not all in the same file. Put all of your recorded audio files in a folder.

3. Select and edit the images you will use in your story

You can find images in many places: taken with a digital camera, scanned with a scanner, or found on the Internet. Most cell phones have cameras that work very well for digital storytelling. You don't need really high-quality images (under 2 megapixels works fine).

You should use a program to crop your images and fix the color and contrast. The preferred program is Photoshop Elements. However, a simple program such as Graphic Convertor would also work. Place your final images into a folder. You could use the same folder as the audio clips, or set up another folder.

iMovie users: The easiest way to import images should begin with organizing them in iPhoto (rather than folders), where you can then see them in the Media tab. You can also use iPhoto to crop and edit your images, and select the specific files you want to create an album for only those pictures that you have selected for your story. Use the album to organize the pictures in the order that you will want to use them in your story.

4. Combine the sound and the images together in a video editing program

Using iMovie for Macintosh, I recommend the following sequence of activities:

1. Import your audio clips in order. Usually, you will need to place the cursor on the timeline where you want the audio to be placed.
2. Import the still images and place them on the timeline on the video track. Match them up to the audio track, changing the duration (length) of the still image.
3   iMovie users: as you import images, apply the "Ken Burns effect" (panning and zooming in on still images) as you place the image on the timeline (preview first).
4. Transitions often change the timing of your images, so you might want to insert the transitions.
5. Create a rough edit (place your narration, soundtrack, and images on the timeline in approximate locations).

iMovie users: Wait to apply very much of the "Ken Burns effect" to images until the next step. Show your movie to someone else and ask for feedback.

6. Insert background music, titles, effects.
7. Do a polish or final edit (ask for final feedback).
8. Export your movie to a playable format.

Adapted from electronicportfolios.com/digistory/howto.html

SCRIPT TEMPLATE FOR A DIGITAL STORY

When writing your script, keep in mind:

Who is the audience for my story?
What is my dramatic question?

When planning your storyboard, keep in mind:

What is the most important thing for my audience to be seeing at this point in time?

Script (narration or audio in video)	Images or Video action	Sound effects, music

Personal Reflection for Digital Narrative Project

We have just completed our digital narrative project. Write a paragraph on the process of creating your narrative. What did you find easy? What did you find difficult?

How did you feel watching your classmates' narratives? What similarities did you notice? What were some common themes? How did this project unite us as a class community? Who would benefit from seeing this group project?

CBAE Proposal by Buffy Kirby

Unit Title: Life Story Banners and Mural for School Building

OBJECTIVE:

Using identity mapping as my primary source and basis for information-gathering with the children, I will conduct group and individual interviews, using the following universal themes to talk about:

Their families—Mom, Dad, sisters, brothers, extended family
Their friends
Favorite colors, foods
What they like to do; what is fun
What they like about their village/town/community; what they don't like
Their faith

From these discussions, we will develop story banners depicting life stories, using burlap (a forgiving printing medium that beautifully portrays texture and dimension), felt, beads, yarn, buttons, natural materials, and prints using local flora and foliage.

We will also learn and talk about some of the traditional African symbols used in fiber and needlework and the adinkra cloth, meaning "artistic beauty." Emphasis will be placed on community ownership, encouraging the children to feel they are a part of making their school beautiful while telling their stories on banners to be hung in the new classroom. These banners will be created with each grade level and as a prelude to the mural project, which will incorporate their stories on the school's exterior wall.

The exterior classroom wall of the school is approximately 12' high by 25' wide, with feasible workspace to reach and develop a mural 8' high by 25' wide. Plans are to work by age group/grade level (height components), sectioning off the project, beginning drawings at the lowest, ground level with the 3rd-grade students and moving upward by section and age/grade level through the 8th-grade class. Each student will have an approximate 15"–20" space within which to depict their story, to "speak their heart in art."

Preparation for the mural painting will involve the community of students, as they will need to assist with scrubbing and priming the wall. I think this will be a wonderful hands-on transition to speaking out their stories from banners—sewing, weaving, printing—to paint!

RATIONALE:

To engage students in their community through art.

I was inspired by a quote I came across in my research from an artist who is part of the Precita Eyes Muralists in San Francisco, California:

> A mural is a bridge to the community. The artists communicate with the people; meetings are held to discuss the issues. The result is a reflection—a mirror of that community.

BUDGET/MATERIALS

According to my research on mural techniques, the most effective paint to use on exterior walls for murals is acrylic latex, alongside natural brushes to get the best detail and texture. The acrylic mural paint should be water-resistant, bright, multipurpose, nontoxic, and mixable and should clean up with soap and water. Several important precautions, "technique facts," were recommended:

1. A primer paint for murals that is durable, resists mold and stains, and is fast-drying is recommended. These paints average $20.00 per gallon (300 square-foot-coverage area); approximately 4 gallons would be needed for safe coverage at a total cost of $80.00.
2. Use "natural" brushes, in a variety of sizes, to penetrate wall textures. These cost $180 for a set of 12 brushes (approximately 6 sets would be needed at a total cost of $1,000).
3. Mapping and taping of assigned areas for painting was recommended, maximizing space and individual artistic opportunity.

I will be denoting needed supplies for this project, and many of the necessary supplies will, I hope, come from donations, such as felt, burlap, sewing implements and notions. Materials to be purchased will likely be the mural primer, paint, and brushes. I hope to raise funds for an additional 6 sewing machines to complement those on site at the school. A further goal for me will be that of introducing the children to the experience of sewing on machines.

If monies and materials allow, I would like to add a printmaking component to my proposal, that of using native sand and plaster of paris to create keepsake footprints with the students. I was intrigued by this project, referenced in an article among my research. After researching this technique, I felt it would add even further to the ownership emphasis within my project. Additional funding would be in the form of 10 5-pound buckets of Crayola (or similar) Air-Dry Clay. The cost would be $12.00 per bucket ($120.00 total for the project). Students would leave their permanent footprints around the school grounds and below the mural!

OUTCOME:

At the conclusion of this proposal and the completion of the mural project, I hope to involve the community/village in an art exhibition, hung and narrated by the students themselves. This is where I will evaluate transformative learning, community involvement, and success as measured by participation and ownership. As several of my bibliographies reflect, I believe that "art is a universal language," that "you can't really fail at making art." Thus, my success measures will be those of community aesthetics and in the personal accomplishments, community involvement, and excitement among my students and the village residents.

CONCLUDING REMARKS:

I chose *The Keeping Quilt*, an illustrated children's book by Patricia Polacco, to guide my proposal, "The Heart 'Speaks' Art." I felt that this beautiful children's story exemplifies the wide-reaching principles of transformation, identity mapping, and an appreciation for our life stories and experiences emphasized throughout my readings and research.

References

Adams, D., & Goldbard, A. (1995). New Deal cultural programs: Experiments in cultural democracy. *Webster's World of Cultural Democracy*. Retrieved from www.wwcd.org/policy/US/newdeal.html

Adejumo, C. O. (2000). Community-based art. *School Arts, 99*(6), 12–13.

Anderson, T., & Milbrandt, M. K. (2005). *Art for life: Authentic instruction in art*. New York, NY: McGraw-Hill.

Andrews, G. (2000). A new vision of aging in the 21st century. *Growing in numbers, growing in strength: Aging a special report*. Urban Age (Winter). United Nations.

Arts Victoria. (2013). Making art with communities—A work guide [Brochure]. Retrieved from creative.vic.gov.au/funding-and-support/resources/making-art-with-communities-a-work-guide

Assam, A. (2009). Why creativity now? A conversation with Sir Ken Robinson. *Educational Leadership, 67*(1), 22–26.

Aston, J. (2001). Research as relationship. In A. L. Cole & J. G. Knowles (Eds.), *Lives in context: The art of life history research* (pp. 145–151). Lanham, MD: AltaMira Press.

Bandura, A. (2002). Social cognitive theory in cultural context. *Applied Psychology: An International Review, 51*(2), 269–290.

Barone, T., & Eisner, E. (2011). *Arts-based research*. Thousand Oaks, CA: Sage.

Bastos, F. (2002). Making the familiar strange: A framework for CBAE practice. In Y. Gaudelius and P. Speirs (Eds.), *Contemporary issues in art education* (pp. 70–83). Upper Saddle River, NJ: Prentice Hall.

Beattie, D. K. (1997). *Assessment in art education*. Worcester, MA: Davis Publications.

Benham, B. (1979). Curriculum theory in the 1970s: The reconceptualist movement. *Journal of Curriculum Theorizing, 3*(1), 162–169.

Blaikie, F. (2014). Arts-informed research: A visual and poetic inquiry into the aesthetics of scholarship. In K. M. Miraglia & C. Smilan (Eds.), *Inquiry in action: Paradigms, methodologies, and perspectives in art education research* (pp. 239–247). Reston, VA: National Art Education Association.

Borwick, D. (2012). *Building communities, not audiences: The future of arts in the United States*. Winston-Salem, NC: ArtsEngaged.

Bresler, L. (1994). Zooming in on the qualitative paradigm in art education: Educational criticism, ethnography and action research. *Visual Arts Research, 19*(1), 30–46.

Bresler, L. (2014). "Seeing as" versus "seeing more": Cultivating connections in arts-based research. In K. M. Miraglia & C. Smilan (Eds.), *Inquiry in action: Paradigms, methodologies, and perspectives in art education research* (pp. 218–226). Reston, VA: National Art Education Association.

Buffington, M. L. (2007). Service-learning and art education. *Art Education, 60*(6), 40–45.

Buffington, M. L. (2014). Power play: Rethinking roles in the art classroom. *VCU Art Education Publications, Paper 7.* scholarscompass.vcu.edu/arte_pubs/7

Burton, D. (2006). *Exhibiting student art: The essential guide for teachers.* New York, NY: Teachers College Press.

Burton, J. M. (1980a). Developing minds: The beginnings of artistic language. *School Arts, 80*(1), 6–12.

Burton, J. M. (1980b). Developing minds: The first visual symbols. *School Arts, 80*(2), 60–65.

Burton, J. M. (1980c). Developing minds: Visual events. *School Arts, 80*(3), 58–64.

Burton, J. M. (1980d). Developing minds: Representing experience from imagination and observation. *School Arts, 80*(4), 26–30.

Burton, J. M. (1981). Developing minds: Representing experiences: Ideas in search of forms. *School Arts, 80*(5), 58–64.

Carter, J. (2018). *The paintings of Jimmy Carter.* Macon, GA: Mercer University Press.

Christiansen, H. (Ed.). (1997). *Recreating relationships: Collaboration and education reform.* Albany, NY: State University of New York Press.

Clandinin, D. J., & Connelly, F. M. (2000). *Narrative inquiry: Experience and story in qualitative research.* San Francisco, CA: Jossey-Bass.

Cohen, G. (2000). *Creative age: Awakening the human potential in the second half of life.* New York, NY: HarperCollins.

Cohen, G. (2005). *The mature mind: The positive power of the aging brain.* New York, NY: Basic Books.

Cole, A. L., & Knowles, J. G. (Eds.). (2001). *Lives in context: The art of life history research.* Lanham, MD: AltaMira Press.

Cole, A. L., & Knowles, J. G. (Eds.). (2008). *Handbook of the arts in qualitative research: Perspectives, methodologies, examples and issues.* Thousand Oaks, CA: Sage.

Cole, A. L., Neilsen, L., Knowles, J. G., & Luciani, T. (Eds.). (2004). *Provoked by art: Theorizing arts-informed inquiry* (Vol. 2). Halifax, Nova Scotia, Canada: Backalong Books.

Congdon, K. (2004). *Community art in action.* Worcester, MA: Davis Publications.

Congdon, K., Blandy, D., & Bolin, P. (Eds.). (2001). *Histories of community-based art education.* Reston, VA: National Art Education Association.

Conle, C. (2003). An anatomy of narrative curricula. *Educational Researcher, 32*(3), 3–15.

Crane, L. (2012). The arts as community citizen. In D. Borwick (Ed.), *Building communities, not audiences: The future of arts in the United States* (pp. 83–91). Winston-Salem, NC: ArtsEngaged.

Cranton, P. (1994). *Understanding and promoting transformative learning: A guide for educators of adults.* San Francisco, CA: Jossey-Bass.

Csikszentmihalyi, M. (1975). *Beyond boredom and anxiety.* San Francisco: Jossey-Bass.

Csikszentmihalyi, M. (1996). *Creativity: Flow and the psychology of discovery and invention.* New York, NY: Harper Perennial.

Csikszentmihalyi, M. (2009). *Flow: The psychology of optimal experience.* New York, NY: HarperCollins.

Daniel, V., & Drew, D. (2011). Art education and the community act: An inquiry into the interior of the process. In B. Young (Ed.), *Art, culture and ethnicity* (2nd ed.; pp. 37–43). Reston, VA: National Art Education Association.

Dewey, J. (1938). *Experience and education.* New York, NY: Collier Books.

Dorfman, D. (1998). *Mapping community assets workbook. Strengthening community education: The basis for sustainable renewal.* Portland, OR: Northwest Regional Educational Lab. (ERIC Document Reproduction Service No. ED426499)

Efland, A. D. (1990). *A history of art education: Intellectual and social currents in teaching the visual arts.* New York, NY: Teachers College Press.

Eisner, E. (2002). *The arts and the creation of mind.* New Haven, CT: Yale University Press.

Eisner, E. (2006). Does arts-based research have a future? Inaugural lecture for the first European conference on arts-based research: Belfast, Northern Ireland, June 2005. *Studies in Art Education: A Journal of Issues and Research in Art Education, 48*(1), 9–18.

Erikson, E. H. (1959). *Identity and the life cycle.* New York, NY: W.W. Norton & Company.

Erikson, E. H., Erikson, J., & Kivnick, H. (1986). *Vital involvement in old age.* New York, NY: W.W. Norton & Company.

Fehr, D., Fehr, K., & Keifer-Boyd, K. (Eds.). (2000). *Real world readings in art education: Things your professors never told you.* New York, NY: Routledge.

Fisher, D., & Frey, N. (2014). *Checking for understanding: Formative assessment techniques for your classroom* (2nd ed.). Alexandria, VA: Association for Supervision and Curriculum Development.

Florence, N. (1998). *bell hooks' engaged pedagogy: A transgressive education for critical consciousness.* Westport, CT: Bergin & Garvey.

Foer, J. S. (2005). *Extremely Loud & Incredibly Close.* Boston, MA: Mariner.

Freire, P. (1970). *Pedagogy of the oppressed.* New York, NY: Herder and Herder.

Furco, A. (1996). Service-learning: A balanced approach to experiential education. In B. Taylor (Ed.), *Expanding boundaries: Serving and learning* (pp. 2–6). Washington, DC: Corporation for National Service.

Gay, G. (2010). *Culturally responsive teaching: Theory, research, and practice* (2nd ed.). New York, NY: Teachers College Press.

Gill, P. (Ed). (2001). *The public library service: IFLA/UNESCO guidelines for development* (IFLA Publications 97). Munich, Germany: K.G. Saur. Retrieved from www.ifla. org/files/assets/hq/publications/archive/the-public-library-service/publ97.pdf

Golden, J., Rice, R., & Kinney, Y. (2003). *Philadelphia murals and the stories they tell.* Philadelphia, PA: Temple University Press.

Gude, O. (2004). Postmodern principles: In search of a 21st century art education. *Art Education, 57*(1), 6–14.

Gude, O. (2007). Principles of possibility: Considerations for a 21st-century art & culture curriculum. *Art Education, 60*(1), 6–17.

Gude, O. (2010). Playing, creativity, possibility. *Art Education, 63*(2), 31–37. doi: 10.1080/00043125.2010.11519059

Guilford, J. P. (1967). *The nature of human intelligence.* New York, NY: McGraw-Hill.

Guskey, T. R. (2000a). *Evaluating professional development.* Thousand Oaks, CA: Corwin.

Haedicke, S. C. (2016). Interrupting a legacy of hatred: Friches Théâtre Urbain's "Lieu Commun." *Research in Drama Education, 21*(2), 161–175.

Hafeli, M. (2014). *Exploring studio materials: Teaching creative art making to children.* New York, NY: Oxford University Press.

Harris, J. (1991). Nationalizing art: The community art centre programme of the federal art project 1935–1943. *Art History, 14*(2), 250–270.

Hatch, J. A., & Wisniewski, R. (Eds.). (1995). *Life history and narrative.* London, UK: Falmer Press.

Helguera, P. (2011). *Education for socially engaged art: A materials and techniques handbook.* New York, NY: Jorge Pinto Books.

Hetland, L., Winner, E., Veenema, S., & Sheridan, K. M. (2013). *Studio thinking 2: The real benefits of visual arts education.* New York, NY: Teachers College Press.

Hoffman, D. H. (1992). *Arts for older adults: An enhancement of life.* Englewood Cliffs, NJ: Prentice Hall.

hooks, b. (1990). *Yearning: Race, gender and cultural politics.* Boston, MA: South End Press.

hooks, b. (1994). *Teaching to transgress: Education as the practice of freedom.* New York, NY: Routledge.

hooks, b. (1995). *Art on my mind: Visual politics.* New York, NY: The New Press.

Howard, D. S. (1973). *The WPA and federal relief policy.* New York, NY: Da Capo Press.

Huber, J., Caine, V., Huber, M., & Steeves, P. (2013). Narrative inquiry as pedagogy in education: The extraordinary potential of living, telling, retelling, and reliving stories of experience. *Review of Research in Education, 37,* 212–242.

Irwin, R. L., & de Cosson, A. (2004). *A/r/tography: Rendering self through arts-based living inquiry.* Vancouver, Canada: Pacific Educational Press.

Jeffers, C. S. (2005). *Spheres of possibility: Linking service-learning and the visual arts.* Reston, VA: National Art Education Association.

Keifer-Boyd, K. (2000). By the people: A community based art curriculum. In D. Fehr, K. Fehr, and K. Keifer-Boyd (Eds.), *Real world readings in art education: Things your professors never told you* (pp. 155–165). New York, NY: Routledge.

Kemmis, S., & McTaggart, R. (1988/1998). *The action research planner.* Geelong, Victoria, Australia: Deakin University Press.

Kim, H. (2015). Community and art: Creative education fostering resilience through art. *Asia Pacific Education Review, 16,* 193–201.

Knight, K., & Schwarzman, M. (2006). *Beginner's guide to community-based arts.* Oakland, CA: New Village Press.

Knowles, M. S. (1975). *Self-directed learning: A guide for learners and teachers.* New York, NY: Association Press.

Kolb, D. A. (1984). *Experiential learning: Experience as the source of learning and development.* Upper Saddle River, NJ: Prentice Hall.

Koster, R. (2011, September 10). The Day Arts/Up close and personal with Jonathan Safran Foer. *The Day.* Retrieved from www.theday.com/article/20110910/ENT03/309109996

Krensky, B., & Steffen, S. L. (2009). *Engaging classrooms and communities through art: A guide to designing and implementing community-based art education.* Lanham, MD: AltaMira Press.

Ladson-Billings, G. (2009). *The dreamkeepers: Successful teachers of African-American children* (2nd ed.). San Francisco, CA: Jossey-Bass.

LaPorte, A. M. (Ed.). (2004). *Community connections: Intergenerational links in art education.* Reston, VA: National Art Education Association.

Lave, J., & Wenger, E. (1991). *Situated learning: Legitimate peripheral participation.* Cambridge, UK: Cambridge University Press.

Lawrence-Lightfoot, S., & Davis, J. H. (1997). *The art and science of portraiture.* San Francisco, CA: Jossey-Bass.

Lawton, P. H. (2004a). Artstories: Exploring intergenerational learning connections through narrative construction. In A. M. La Porte (Ed.), *Community connections: Intergenerational links in art education* (pp. 29–44). Reston, VA: National Art Education Association.

Lawton, P. H. (2004b). *Artstories: Perspectives on intergenerational learning through narrative construction amongst adolescents, middle aged and older aged adults* (Unpublished doctoral dissertation). Teachers College, New York.

Lawton, P. H. (2010). Hand-in-hand: Building community on common ground. *Art Education, 63*(6), 6–12.

Lawton, P. H. (2014). The role of art education in cultivating community and leadership through creative collaboration. *Visual Inquiry: Learning & Teaching Art, 3*(3), 421–436.

Lawton, P. H. (2017). Curate¹, curate²|curator¹, curator²: Curatorial practice in art education. *Visual Inquiry: Learning & Teaching Art, 6*(1), 95–105.

Lawton, P. H., & La Porte, A. M. (2013). Beyond traditional art education: Transformative lifelong learning in community-based settings with older adults. *Studies in Art Education: A Journal of Issues and Research in Art Education, 54*(4), 310–320.

Lewin, K. (1958). *Group decision and social change.* New York, NY: Holt, Rinehart and Winston.

London, P. (1994). *Step outside: Community-based art education.* Portsmouth, NH: Heinemann.

Lowenfeld, V. (1947/1952). *Creative and mental growth* (2nd ed.). New York, NY: Macmillan.

Luehrman, M., & Unrath, K. (2006). Making theories of children's artistic development meaningful for pre-service teachers. *Art Education, 59*(3), 6–12.

Matarasso, F. (1997). *Use or ornament? The social impact of participation in the arts.* Stroud, UK: Comedia. Retrieved from www.creativenz.govt.nz/assets/ckeditor/attachments/1033/francois_matarasso_use_or_ornament.pdf?1410238133.

May, W. (1993). Teachers as researchers or action research: What is it and what good is it for art education? *Studies in Art Education: A Journal of Issues and Research in Art Education, 34*(2), 114–126.

McKernan, J. (1996). *Curriculum action research: A handbook of methods and resources for the reflective practitioner.* London, UK: Kogan Page Ltd.

McKnight, J. L., & Kretzmann, J. P. (1993). *Building communities from the inside out: A path toward finding and mobilizing a community's assets.* Chicago, IL: ACTA Publications.

McTighe, J. (2004). *Understanding by design: Professional development workbook.* Alexandria, VA: Association for Supervision and Curriculum Development.

Mezirow, J. (1990). *Fostering critical reflection in adulthood.* San Francisco, CA: Jossey-Bass.

Mezirow, J. (1991). *Transformative dimensions of adult learning.* San Francisco, CA: Jossey-Bass.

Michael, J. A. (Ed.). (1982). *The Lowenfeld lectures.* University Park, PA: Pennsylvania State University Press.

Michelson, E. (2015). *Gender, experience, and knowledge in adult learning: Alisoun's daughters.* New York, NY: Routledge.

Milner, H. R. (2013). Analyzing poverty, learning, and teaching through a critical race theory lens. *Review of Research in Education, 37,* 1–53.

Miraglia, K. M., & Smilan, C. (Eds.). (2014). *Inquiry in action: Paradigms, methodologies, and perspectives in art education research.* Reston, VA: National Art Education Association.

Morales, L. (2010, November 15). Social offerings, openness key to community attachment. *Gallup.* Retrieved from news.gallup.com/poll/144476/social-offerings-openness-key-community-attachment.aspx.

Newman, T., Curtis, K., & Stephens, J. (2001). Do community-based art projects result in social gains? A review of the literature. *Community Development Journal, 38*(3), 10–22.

Nussbaum, M. (1997). *Cultivating humanity: A classical defense of reform in liberal education.* Cambridge, MA: Harvard University Press.

Oakes, J., Lipton, M., Anderson, L., & Stillman, J. (2018). *Teaching to change the world.* New York, NY: Routledge.

Paley, N. (1996). *Finding art's place: Experiments in contemporary education and culture.* New York, NY: Routledge.

Perkins, D. (1993). Teaching for understanding. *American Educator: The Professional Journal of the American Federation of Teachers, 17*(3), 28–35.

Pinar, W. (1975). *Curriculum theorizing: The reconceptualists.* Berkley, CA: McCutchan.

Polacco, P. (1998). *The keeping quilt.* New York, NY: Simon & Schuster Books for Young Readers.

Prigoff, J., & Dunitz, R. (2000). *Walls of heritage, walls of pride: African American murals.* Rohnert Park, CA: Pomegranate Books.

Putnam, R. (2000). *Bowling alone: The collapse and revival of American community.* New York, NY: Simon & Schuster.

Richards, S. B., Frank, C. L., Sableski, M., & Arnold, J. M. (2016). *Collaboration among professionals, students, families and communities: Effective teaming for student learning.* New York, NY: Routledge.

Russell, R L., & Hutzel, K. (2007). Promoting social and emotional learning through service-learning art projects. *Art Education, 60*(3), 6–11.

Santrock, J. W. (2010). *Life-span development* (13th ed.). New York, NY: McGraw-Hill.

Simpson, J. W., Delaney, J. M., Carroll, K. L., Hamilton, C. M, Kay, S. I., Kerlavage, M. S., & Olson, J. L. (1998). *Creating meaning through art: Teacher as choice maker*. Upper Saddle River, NJ: Prentice Hall.

Stewart, M. G., & Walker, S. R. (2005). *Rethinking curriculum in art*. Worcester, MA: Davis Publications.

Stiggins, R. (2007). Assessment through the students' eyes. *Educational Leadership, 64*(8), 22–26.

Sullivan, G. (2010). *Art practice as research: Inquiry in visual arts* (2nd ed.). Thousand Oaks, CA: Sage.

Taylor, E. W. (1998). *The theory and practice of transformative learning: A critical review*. Columbus, OH: Ohio State University. (ERIC Document Reproduction Service No. RR93002001)

Taylor, E. W. (2008). Transformative learning theory. *New Directions for Adult and Continuing Education, 119*, 5–15.

Taylor, P. G., and Ballengee-Morris, C. (2004). Service-Learning: A language of "we." *Art Education, 57*(5), 6–12.

Tisdell, E. J. (2003). *Exploring spirituality and culture in adult and higher education*. San Francisco, CA: Jossey-Bass.

Tisdell, E. J., & Tolliver, D. E. (2001). The role of spirituality in culturally relevant and transformative adult education. *Adult Learning, 12*(3), 13–14.

Tomlinson, C. A., & McTighe, J. (2006). *Integrating differentiated instruction and understanding by design*. Alexandria, VA: Association for Supervision and Curriculum Instruction.

Torrance, E. P. (1965). *Rewarding creative behavior: Experiments in classroom creativity*. Englewood Cliffs, NJ: Prentice Hall.

Triggs, V., Irwin, R. L., & O'Donoghue, D. (2014). Following a/r/tography in practice: From possibility to potential. In K. M. Miraglia & C. Smilan (Eds.), *Inquiry in action: Paradigms, methodologies, and perspectives in art education research* (pp. 253–261). Reston, VA: National Art Education Association.

Trolander, J. A. (1975). *Settlement houses and the Great Depression*. Detroit, MI: Wayne State University Press.

Ulbricht, J. (2005). What is community-based art education? *Art Education, 58*(2), 6–12.

VanderVen, K. (1999). Intergenerational theory: The missing element in today's intergenerational programs. In V. S. Kuehne (Ed.), *Intergenerational programs: Understanding what we have created* (pp. 33–47). New York, NY: Haworth Press.

Vygotsky, L. S. (1978). *Mind and society: The development of higher order psychological processes*. Cambridge, MA: Harvard University Press.

Walker, M. A. (2018) The unity mural: Bridging communities through artmaking. *International Journal of Lifelong Learning in Art Education, 1*(6). Retrieved from scholarscompass.vcu.edu/ijllae/vol1/iss1/6

Walker, S. R. (2001). *Teaching meaning in artmaking* (Art Education in Practice series). Worcester, MA: Davis Publications.

Walker, S. (2004). Big ideas: Understanding the art making process—Reflective practice. *Art Education, 57*(3), 6–12.

Wallas, G. (1925). *The art of thought*. New York, NY: Harcourt Brace.

Watkins, E., & Gangel, J. (2017, February 27). George W. Bush discovers his "inner Rembrandt" in homage to veterans. *CNN Politics*. Retrieved from www.cnn.com/2017/02/27/politics/george-w-bush-paintings/index.html

White, B. (2010) Power, privilege, and the public: The dynamics of community–university collaboration. *New Directions for Higher Education, 152*, 67–74.

Wilson, B., & Wilson, M. (1982). *Teaching children to draw: A guide for teachers and parents*. Englewood Cliffs, NJ: Prentice Hall.

Wilson, C. (2016). Is our maximum lifespan 115? *New Scientist, 232*(3094), 10.

Wrightsman, L. (1994). *Adult personality development*. Thousand Oaks, CA: Sage.

WTTW Chicago, PBS. Allen, B.E. and Andries, D. (Producers). (2010, June 15). *DuSable to Obama, Chicago's black metropolis: Power, politics & pride*. AfriCOBRA. Retrieved from www.wttw.com/main.taf?p=76,4,5,9.

Index

Note: A page number followed by *f* indicates figures and other illustrative material.

About the Authors

Pamela Harris Lawton, MFA, Ed D.C.T.A., a fifth-generation educator, native of Washington, DC, and practicing artist, is associate professor of art education at Virginia Commonwealth University. Her artistic and scholarly research, Art-stories, revolves around visual narrative and intergenerational arts learning in community settings. In addition to publishing a monograph on her dissertation research, *Artstories: Narrative Construction in Intergenerational and Transformative Learning* (2008), Pamela has published several book chapters and journal articles and served as founder/senior editor of the peer-reviewed *International Journal of Lifelong Learning in Art Education*. Her artworks are in the following collections: College of Health and Human Services, University of North Carolina at Charlotte; Morgan State University; Georgetown University; The Corcoran School of the Arts + Design/George Washington University; Frederick Douglass Museum and Cultural Center; Eugene E. Myers Charitable Remainders Trust; Washington, DC, Superior Court; Cabell Library artists books collection at Virginia Commonwealth University; Teachers College, Columbia University; Northwestern University; University of North Dakota; and the University of West Virginia. In 2019, Pamela received a prestigious U.S./UK Fulbright Commission Distinguished Chair/Visiting Professorship to conduct Artstories research at the University of Edinburgh. She was selected as the second U.S. associate artist to conduct a week-long community-based art project in the Tate Modern Exchange program. In addition, she is an elected member of the Council of Policy Studies in Art Education, a select group of art educators founded by Eliot Eisner. Learn more about Pamela's work at pamelaspress.wixsite.com/artstories.

Margaret A. Walker, EdD, has been an artist and educator in a variety of community, school, museum, and university settings. In New York City, she taught studio art at Lexington School for the Deaf and at the Educational Alliance Art School. Margaret worked as an educator at the Noguchi Museum and taught art education courses at Adelphi University. She now teaches in the art education program at the University of Maryland, College Park, as well as coordinating the master's programs in Visual Arts and Arts Integration in UMD's College of Education. Margaret holds an EdD in Art and Art Education from Columbia University's Teachers College, where the focus of her dissertation work was the role that artmaking plays in critical thinking and adolescent identity development. Her most recent publications examine the links between theory and practice in studio teaching, and community-based artmaking as a source of healing after a tragedy upended a community.

Together with Pamela Lawton and Melissa Green, Margaret has taught community-based art education courses in Washington, DC, and Maryland. Her most recent community mural collaboration with Bowie State University's studio art program is touring the state of Maryland, and she directs an ongoing social justice postcard project, the Artivist Postcard Collective. Margaret is a painter and fiber/mixed-media artist who has recently exhibited work in New York City, Alexandria, VA, and Baltimore, MD. She lives with her husband, daughter, cat, and occasional wildlife on the border of DC and MD.

Melissa Green has a passion for building community through collaborative, interdisciplinary, and socially engaged creative practice. For over 10 years she has worked as a museum educator, artist, and creative community engagement designer. As the Director of Community Partnerships at the Corcoran Gallery of Art and later as Executive Director of ArtReach and the Community Gallery at Town Hall Education, Arts, and Recreation Campus (THEARC), Melissa managed the ArtReach programs, exhibitions, collaborative projects, and outreach initiatives for underserved communities in Washington, DC. In her work, she enjoys forging cross-cultural connections in art and transforming communities through creative and accessible place-making initiatives. During her time at ArtReach, the program developed into one of the most respected youth arts programs in the District and worked with such organizations as the Smithsonian's Freer Gallery, the National Park Service, the Eleventh Street Bridge Park Project, the District Department of the Environment, Art in Embassies, and the Office of the State Superintendent of Education. Green also spearheaded the development of the ArtReach Master Class and Visiting Artist Program, which led to students participating in projects with renowned artists such as Nina Chanel Abney, Nick Cave, Mia Feuer, and David Levinthal. In 2010, ArtReach was selected for the President's Committee on the Arts and Humanities First Lady's annual service project and worked with Michelle Obama on a youth mural project. In 2013, ArtReach was awarded the Mayor's Arts Award for Innovation in the Arts. In addition to her work with ArtReach, Melissa taught community and museum arts engagement courses at George Washington University and the Corcoran College of Art + Design and served as Director of Youth Programming and Continuing Education at the Corcoran. Prior to moving to Washington, DC, Green taught art and design courses in Chicago. She received her Master of Arts in Teaching from the Corcoran College of Art + Design. Learn more about Melissa's community work at www.greencommunitycreative.com.